PRAISE FOR *THE ROOTED RENEGADE*

"*The Rooted Renegade* presents a compelling, accessible approach to personal growth, helping readers level up their lives and, ultimately, create a lasting legacy. Author Rebecca Arnold offers relatable stories combined with practical step-by-step guidance. The book provides an overall framework that was new to me—and very helpful in seeing the bigger picture of what matters most in our lives.

Arnold's insights into human nature, combined with her empathetic spirit, make each chapter a delight. As a reader, I felt the author was reaching out to me as a wise and supportive friend, offering expert guidance so I could better navigate life's complexities."

—**BJ Fogg, PhD,** author of *New York Times* bestseller *Tiny Habits*; founder, Stanford University Behavior Design Lab

"As a social-impact leader, it is vital to do the inner work that supports transformational impact. *The Rooted Renegade* is a powerful guidebook to do just that. It walks you step-by-step through fostering a bedrock sense of internal peace and calm, forging a deeper relationship with yourself in service of authenticity, and clarifying your legacy in order to see through the changes you envision in your communities."

—**Maria Flynn,** president and CEO, Jobs for the Future (JFF)

"Save your money by reading *The Rooted Renegade!* You don't need an expensive week at a spa, generous donations to a spiritual guide or religion, or expensive mood-altering substances. Rebecca Arnold has amassed the Guidebook to Inner Peace. The vast array of exercises offers a lot of possibilities. I suspect you need only one or two of them to really hit home and help you center and reconnect with your sense of purpose and love, and with life-giving relationships."

—**Richard Boyatzis, PhD,** distinguished university professor, Case Western Reserve University; coauthor of *Helping People Change* and the international bestseller *Primal Leadership*

"In these times of great uncertainty and change, the teachings in this book are essential. *The Rooted Renegade* maps three key components of peace, providing clear pathways and potent practices to help you level up your capacity and ground in your peace."

—**Joel Monk,** cofounder, Coaches Rising

"*The Rooted Renegade* is a pivotal resource for both coaches and leaders who want to deepen their impact and navigate the complexities of personal and professional growth. Rebecca Arnold's approach blends profound insights with a broad range of practical exercises to achieve internal, existential, and relational peace. For coaches, this book will serve to enrich your practice, offering a rich tool kit for facilitating transformative dialogues, enabling clients to unlock their potential. For leaders and high-achieving individuals, this is an easy-to-follow road map to achieve fulfillment, improve relationships (at work and at home), and create a legacy."

—**Rachel Goldstein, MBA, CPCC, PCC,**
executive coach and facilitator at Harvard Business School, Chief, and The Leadership Consortium

"It took a cancer diagnosis for me to let go of unhelpful and self-limiting mindsets about what it means to be a successful executive. Fortunately, you don't have to experience a health crisis to build a more peaceful, meaningful, and joyful life. Rebecca Arnold has written a beautiful, deeply-felt guide to align your work with your strengths, values, and passions—and build the courage to actually execute. I highly recommend this book for leaders seeking greater purpose and meaning in their relationships with themselves and others. In a sea of personal development and leadership books, *The Rooted Renegade* stands out."

—**Elena Bernardo,** SVP of Operations at a major food tech company

"In *The Rooted Renegade*, Rebecca Arnold provides a road map to a life filled with joy, purpose, and fulfillment. She has given us a companion on our personal journey that inspires, uplifts, and empowers. Whether you are seeking to overcome challenges, enhance your resilience, or simply savor the joys of everyday life, this book provides the tools and insights you need."

—**Dr. Rebecca Baumgartner,** senior vice president for People and Operations, Greater Kansas City Chamber of Commerce

"Do you want to feel better about yourself, those you love, and those who confound you? Read this book! Rebecca Arnold has a way of cutting to the chase, inviting her readers into a no-nonsense relationship with themselves and those who surround them—all while encouraging self-awareness, generosity of spirit, and whole-hearted living."

—**Christine E. Crouse-Dick, PhD,** cofounder, Slow Leadership Institute; professor of communication arts and faculty dean, Bethel College (KS-US)

"This personal development book does something few do well: It offers infinite gems of wisdom about what's holding us back coupled with simple exercises that, with practice, help us get out of our own way and access peace from the inside out. Rebecca Arnold is not afraid to tackle real struggles such as negative self-talk, self-sabotage, managing criticism, setting boundaries, and finding forgiveness. She does so with raw honesty and compassion and leaves you feeling capable of change and ready to claim your peace."

—**Elisa B. MacDonald,** best-selling author of *Intentional Moves: How Skillful Team Leaders Impact Learning*

"*The Rooted Renegade* strikes the perfect balance of gentle exploration, relatable storytelling, and concrete tools for growth. Rebecca weaves these seamlessly into a book that feels like a cozy chat with a brilliant, wise friend."

—**Amy Johnston, LCSW, PMH-C,** clinical director, Urban Wellness

"With invaluable insights and strategic exercises, *The Rooted Renegade* offers a path for reflection and recalibration. A guide for people at all stages of life, it helps us look at the ingrained habits and narratives that may be blocking us from living more satisfying personal and professional lives. Rebecca's intelligent, warm, and humorous writing makes you feel that she is right there with you—the next best thing to her coaching you in person."

—**Gail Schwartz, EdD,** former senior vice president for Academic, Innovation, and Student Success, American Association of Community Colleges

THE ROOTED
RENEGADE

REBECCA ARNOLD

THE ROOTED RENEGADE

Transform Within, Disrupt the Status Quo & Unleash Your Legacy

GREENLEAF
BOOK GROUP PRESS

The names and identifying characteristics of persons referenced in this book, as well as identifying events and places, have been changed to protect the privacy of the individuals and their families. In some cases, composites of clients are used out of an abundance of caution.

This book is intended as a reference volume only. It is sold with the understanding that the publisher and author are not engaged in rendering any professional services. The material presented is for informational purposes and intended for self-discovery and to broaden your horizons but is not intended for treatment. If you suspect that you have a problem that might require professional treatment or advice, you should seek competent help. If you have experienced trauma, do not engage with the exercises contained herein that could trigger your trauma, and seek professional care as needed. The author and publisher specifically disclaim all responsibility for any liability, loss, or risk—personal or otherwise—that is incurred as a consequence, directly or indirectly, of the use and application of any of the contents of this book.

Published by Greenleaf Book Group Press
Austin, Texas
www.gbgpress.com

Distributed by Greenleaf Book Group

For ordering information or special discounts for bulk purchases, please contact Greenleaf Book Group at PO Box 91869, Austin, TX 78709, 512.891.6100.

Design and composition by Greenleaf Book Group and Brian Phillips
Cover design by Greenleaf Book Group and Brian Phillips
Cover image ©Stockphoto.com/BlackJack3D

Publisher's Cataloging-in-Publication data is available.

Print ISBN: 979-8-88645-185-6

eBook ISBN: 979-8-88645-186-3

To offset the number of trees consumed in the printing of our books, Greenleaf donates a portion of the proceeds from each printing to the Arbor Day Foundation. Greenleaf Book Group has replaced over 50,000 trees since 2007.

Printed in the United States of America on acid-free paper

24 25 26 27 28 29 30 31   10 9 8 7 6 5 4 3 2 1

First Edition

To P, R, & R,
for the learning and love along the way . . .
also, boatloads of laughter.

CONTENTS

Introduction 1

PART I Generate Internal Peace 13

Chapter One Leverage Your Body's Wisdom 15

Chapter Two Cultivate Peaceful Emotions 35

Chapter Three Harness Self-Talk 61

PART II Catalyze Existential Peace 71

Chapter Four Dance with Mortality 73

Chapter Five Find Your Soul's Water 79

Chapter Six Motivate without Fear 101

PART III Unlock Relational Peace 121

Chapter Seven Discover Your Relationship with Yourself ... 123

Chapter Eight Deepen Your Relationships with Others 163

Chapter Nine Define Your Relationship with the World 185

PART IV Explore the Peace Dojo 193

Chapter Ten Learn from Your Dark Night of the Soul 195

Chapter Eleven Uncover What Remains 203

Conclusion You're a Rooted Renegade Now 215

Acknowledgments 217

Notes 219

About the Author 229

EXERCISES

Introduction

Create Intention 10

PART I | **Generate Internal Peace**

Chapter One

Open Lines of Communication 17

Tap into Your Body's Insights 18

Embody Calm 22

Just Breathe 27

Expand Your Breath 27

Presence Your Body 29

Evoke Your Senses 31

Reflect and Commit 33

Chapter Two

Generate Body Gratitude 40

Harness Your Imagination 42

Identify Your Emotions' Physical Imprints 43

Create Feelings of Abundance 46

Clear Energetic Crud 51

Find Your Tells 54

Bust a Habit 58

Chapter Three

Integrate Positive Self-Talk 68

PART II | Catalyze Existential Peace

Chapter Four

Make Mortality Real 77

Chapter Five

Discover Your Legacy 84

Unmask Genius 89

Name and Claim Strengths 91

Center on Strengths 95

Identify Your Values 97

Chapter Six

Claim Your Wins 104

Rewire Thought-Looping 107

Check Yourself 108

Shake Up Your Perspective 111

Seed Resourcefulness 113

Set Yourself Up for Success 115

Tame Self-Sabotage 117

PART III | Unlock Relational Peace

Chapter Seven

Create Your Life Map 124

Greet Your Wise Essence 129

Ground Your Essence in Place 132

Connect with Essence 133

Name Your Pit Crew 135

Go Deep with Your Pit Crew 138

Reflect on Thriving 142

Know Your Needs, Wants, and Dreams 143

Claim Your Needs, Wants, and Dreams 146

Circle Up and Get Accountable 147

Strengthen Self-Compassion 149

Get Intimate with Your Inner Critic 153

Face the Dragon 156

Visualize Next-Gen You 159

Chapter Eight

Identify Your Tender Spots 165

Understand How Criticism Works in You 168

Make Boundaries Real 172

Audit Relationships 174

Reinvent Relationships 178

Forge Forgiveness 181

Chapter Nine

Explore Your Relationships with Universal Ideas 188

Embrace Perspectives on the World 190

PART IV | Explore the Peace Dojo

Chapter Ten

Mine Your Dark Night of the Soul 200

INTRODUCTION

What *Is* a "Rooted Renegade"?

Most of us are caught in the hustle of daily life and use quick fixes to find relief from our stress, overwhelm, and burnout. But when I say, "rooted renegade," I'm talking about those of you who yearn for change from the inside out. At your core, you want a purposeful, authentic life, rather than merely getting through the day. Whether in your workplace, family, relationships, community, or institutions, you seek innovation and impact because the status quo is broken. In a climate of racism, ableism, homophobia, transphobia, and misogyny, you desire a heart-centered life that builds others—and yourself—up. Amid capitalistic values and an ultracompetitive world, you recognize that true, holistic success begins inside. And you understand this work requires a sense of humor, a dose of humility, and the courage to try new things, fail, and try again.

Allow what you've just read to activate something within you: passion, commitment, drive, possibility . . .

The approaches and strategies in this book are intended to help you make deep, lasting changes that will improve your well-being and lead you toward holistic success. But what does this mean, practically? Accessing calm during chaos, getting reinvigorated about your work, forging a better balance between work and the rest of your life, creating boundaries so you have more time and energy, building habits and mindsets that fuel you, standing in your values, becoming your own internal support system, and so much more.

To do this, you will learn how to create a solid foundation called *rooted peace* to support you as you shake up *your* world for the good. This rooted peace includes internal peace (using your body, breath, emotions, and thoughts to generate calm, build resilience, and counteract stress), existential peace (discovering and using your legacy, genius, and values), and relational peace (forging a fulfilling relationship with yourself and others and managing conflict in satisfying ways).

You have the capacity to become a rooted renegade. Whether you crave more impact in your life than the daily grind, "have it all" but still feel miserable, believe you can't possibly do what you love, or have tried self-care and vacations but discovered you're unable to turn off work or simply get a break from yourself, I have experienced all of this, and my clients have too. And there's so much more calm, fulfillment, and joy available to you.

Are these changes easy? No. You will be tempted by the easier path of the status quo. You will face self-doubt and frustrations along the way. Yet, by boldly stepping into your gifts, who you truly are, and the audacity of your dreams, you will stand against the shoulds and can'ts that society uses for control and order. To live contrary to norms, even dysfunctional ones, takes extraordinary fortitude and resilience. You will confront doubters and resistance. You will wonder if the journey is worth it as you rewire your old ways of being and confront what's not working in your world. I promise you. It *is* worth it! For disruption seeds healing, within and without.

And there's a lot of healing needed in the world right now.

The extraordinary pace of life and work is untenable. The array of challenges in the world that seem to mount daily are soul-crushing. While living an authentic, purposeful life won't solve everything, it will have ripple effects for your community, your workplace, your relationships, your family, and others around you.

In my practice as a coach for mission-driven leaders in the trenches of fundamental change to our school systems, health-care systems, higher education systems, academic fields, and social-impact organizations, I have seen my clients enjoy dividends from creating a foundation of rooted peace. They have stepped into their legacies and lived in greater alignment with their values. They have transmuted relationships on the brink of rupture. Their chronic illnesses have lightened. Decades of self-beratement have fallen away, replaced by self-compassion. The resilience born from rooted peace has given them the solid footing to shake up their institutions and their lives.

The next frontier of true success in the twenty-first century will be profound, lasting, self-generating peace. Not money. Not fame. Not possessions. Instead, this version of success will look like spaciousness. More time and less hustle. Knowing how to calm your nervous system and fire up your passions to create a deeply fulfilling life on your own terms. This is a countercultural notion, so enjoy the rebellion.

The Three Essential Components of Rooted Peace

When you hear the word *peace*, you likely think about an inner sense of calm, a lack of conflict, an ease and spaciousness. But rooted peace is richer and more nuanced. Imagine you are sitting on a beach, hearing the waves, looking far out to the horizon, smelling the sand and surf. The body is calm and safe and things feel "right." Tranquility is present, fiery emotions are muted, and the softer emotions are louder. You speak to yourself gently and kindly. You're not worrying that you're wasting your life. You're not fretting about a perpetually challenging relationship. This is rooted peace. And it generates a body-mind-heart synergy that's a powerful foundation for living full out.

This comprehensive notion of rooted peace has three spheres: internal, existential, and relational. We seek peace in each of these domains. Therefore, when something feels fundamentally *off* in our lives, we can examine each domain and find ideas for interventions to create greater wholeness. The practical tools and strategies in this book will help you do just that.

Internal peace is the body's felt sense of calm, tranquility, and presence in the moment. There's a soaking-it-all-in quality of relaxation and spaciousness, like a vessel holding vast potential. You can purposefully create internal peace using strategies for your body, thoughts, emotions, and environments. This will help you build greater resilience and counteract stress.

Existential peace comes from connecting with and honoring your purpose. You lean into your gifts fully. You live in integrity with your values, claim your deepest desires, and—in your own unique way—contribute to making the world better. In doing so, you contribute authentically and meaningfully to a purpose that's a full-throated *yes.* You experience profound existential peace and the fulfillment, joy, and balance that comes along with it.

Relational peace is the result of intentionally forging a deep connection with and appreciation of yourself, fostering external relationships that honor your needs and desires, and managing conflict in self-honoring ways.

If we fall short of peace in any of these three aspects, it is difficult to have the whole body-mind-heart experience of rooted peace that we actually crave instead of the temporary fixes we think we do (like streaming television, scrolling social media, and purchasing mindlessly). For example, one client held a leadership position through which he had the power to impact thousands of children's lives for the better. He embodied existential peace: His job had purpose, he honored his values of equity and inclusion, and he was in a position to create change. But his relational peace was in shambles: He was filled with self-recrimination and self-doubt, with self-talk that sounded like, "Why are you such a failure? You can't do anything right. You're letting everyone down." This decimated his relationship with himself, which in turn compromised his physical and emotional well-being. He wrestled with patterns of unhealthy eating, poor sleeping, and a lack of exercise that left him feeling depleted and exhausted.

Another client had her relational peace intact: She spoke to herself kindly for the most part, had fulfilling relationships with her partner and children, and prioritized close friendships. But she floundered when transitioning out of her long-term career field. She wrestled with existential peace, asking herself questions such as: What is my identity now? How will I do work that matters to the world? Will this next phase be enough to fulfill me?

Most of us (myself included!) face challenges in all three domains. This can disrupt our well-being. By prioritizing rooted peace, you can use interventions for each aspect of peace—internal, existential, and relational—to become a more present, centered version of yourself. My invitation to you is not to seek *perfection* in all three areas. Please reread that last sentence. We are all a work in progress and will remain so for our whole lives. My intention is to offer you a lens through which to identify what's working and what's not working in your life and why, and what the heck you can do about it.

If you feel a bit intimidated or reluctant, that's perfectly normal. You're on the brink of shifting things in your life for the better and stretching your comfort zone. This book will guide you step-by-step through these changes. You've got this.

My Journey Inspired This Book

I am an unexpected author for a book centered on rootedness and peace. After all, I haven't lived in a monastery, I haven't meditated every day for the last twenty years, and I don't live a quiet life. But that's exactly why I've written this book. I'm a pretty average person, just like you. I have grumpy teenagers. I yell at crows, curse in traffic, and bite my nails. And yet, the practices I share in this book have enabled me to find peace amid this crazy world and my own personal brand of chaos.

My own journey down this path started six years ago. Looking back, I now understand that all three spheres of rooted peace were in massive disarray. This led to colossal burnout from my dream job as a policy director at an education nonprofit, aiming to make a tectonic impact on education systems and students. My burnout kicked off a period of deep despair. I didn't sleep, I couldn't eat, I couldn't care for my children. Self-hatred crowded out any sense of logic or purpose— or even love. "I'm not good at anything," I told myself. "I'm unlovable, and I've made a mess of my life." I went to a psychiatrist, to a therapist twice a week, to an acupuncturist, to an internist. In between, I lay in bed hoping for something to change through either death, or medicine, or a miracle.

When I finally got the right medicine so that I could sleep and the extreme self-hatred quieted, I entered a phase of healing. That looked like sleeping well, eating healthfully, spending time with my children, and continuing physical and mental health care.

It took two months for me to believe that things could get better. I leaned into the gratitude I felt for my health, my family, and my husband. I began acknowledging my own role in creating my undoing: an extreme lack of boundaries, a massive work-life imbalance that left me depleted and racked with "mom guilt," relationships that sucked me dry, and excessive perfectionism and procrastination that made it hard to do my job sanely. I realized I'd been profoundly disconnected from my body and its signals, which was dangerous given a chronic illness that affects my body's ability to manage and metabolize stress.

After six more months, I began to heal physically and emotionally. I forged honest, deep connections with friends. I began listening to my body. I identified the mindsets and patterns that had started all this trouble in the first place: believing that my only value came from serving others, that I deserved to rest only when everything in my work and home life was perfect, and that my life was worthless unless I made a significant impact. As I began to heal, I started meditating, doing yoga, and exploring Reiki and other alternative healing approaches to release the old patterns that no longer served me. I forged new connections between my body, mind, heart, and spirit.

After a year, my foundation was stable enough that I could ask myself the big questions: What do I want to do with my life *now*? With the demise of my dream job came a vacuum of purpose. I wanted to have an impact on others *while* keeping my work and life in harmony. But doing what?

In college, I studied psychology and loved learning how people tick and how they change. As I wrestled with what to do with my life post-dream job, somewhere deep in my mind a thought bloomed: being a coach could be a good fit. Coaching seemed like an ideal marriage of my interests in psychology and personal development and my commitment to social impact.

Through my training to become a coach, I accelerated my healing. I began to hold myself more gently, to find more joy, and to coach myself through challenges. When I coached practice clients during my training, I got so hot—literally. It was as if my lifeforce and passion merged, heating me up from the inside out. I knew this work would light my soul ablaze.

The essential strategies, practices, and experiences I used to generate peace for myself in my time of direst need served me well in my new career. I learned ways to access the wisdom of my body. I practiced harnessing my thoughts to show up for myself with grace. My coaching practice allowed me to do soul-aligned work, drawing upon my purpose and gifts. Instead of succumbing to ever-shifting moods, I practiced shifting my emotions and the mindsets that fuel them. I changed my habits and patterns and identified supports in the form of people and structures. And you can too! Trust that quiet voice within you that knows you are ready to live differently.

I want you to understand these approaches and ideas so you can prevent your own suffering, enjoy a rooted peace that heals, and create a life on your own terms. We have all experienced challenging seasons of life like I did. We need the skills to come out the other side stronger, clearer, and more aligned with our goals and values than before.

My deepest hope is that the strategies, tools, and resources in this book will support you to make your own life-affirming changes.

How to Use This Book

The Rooted Renegade offers practical guidance that you can implement immediately to help you achieve internal, existential, and relational peace. The strategies are transformative yet simple. They are designed to evoke the wisdom you already possess but may have difficulty accessing in the day-to-day. Take what serves you and leave the rest.

In addition to presenting concepts, theories, and anecdotes, each chapter also presents questions to consider, journaling prompts to expand your thinking, visualizations to awaken your imagination, and practices to experiment with. I invite you to approach these all with a spirit of play, openness, and curiosity.

As you work through the book, it is optimal to complete the exercises in order. Doing so will ensure that you experience the momentum and coherence of each lesson building upon the previous one. And take your time. This is not a "devour and chuck it on the pile" type of book. Consider it essential reference material on your journey to becoming a rooted renegade.

That said, after you've done the exercises once, please make them your own. Consider the exercises to be a menu for you to mix and play with if that's what serves you. I have intentionally organized the content into digestible sections. But feel free to meld content and exercises from different sections. You are fully empowered to make this book work for you! In addition, my website has lots of resources to assist you along the way. Don't hesitate to check them out at www.therootedrenegade.com/resources.

Before you start the first exercise, identify a journal for the activities in the book. Having one place for your thoughts and journaling prompts will help build the muscle memory of reflection. Creating a routine for yourself related to opening and working with this book is another helpful practice. For example, you might take a deep breath and roll your shoulders down and back or feel your feet firmly on the ground. Or perhaps you reread the intention you write in the first exercise whenever you open the book anew.

Moving through this book with a friend or a group may expand your insights beyond your own self-reflections and provide accountability and support as you implement the practices. There's no time like now, so let's get started.

EXERCISE > CREATE INTENTION

Before you begin the next chapter, set an intention. Take three deep breaths in and out, and tune in to that quiet, wise part within you. What do you most want from this book and the experience of reading it? Why did you buy this book in the first place? What peace are you yearning for? Now sit your butt down and get to it.

Write your intention in the following space or in the journal you've chosen.

_____

_____

_____

_____

_____

Takeaways: Introduction

✓ **Rooted peace** has three components: **internal, existential,** and **relational.** Peace in all three areas is necessary for optimum happiness and well-being. You don't have to get it perfect! In fact, don't try to! These are lenses to identify why something feels amiss and what to do about it.

✓ Being a **rooted renegade** means rejecting superficial, external sources of peace (e.g., food, entertainment, possessions) and turning inward to pursue the true, lasting peace that comes with deep reflection and self-knowledge and allows you to shake up the status quo in your life for the better.

✓ You will achieve the best results from this book by taking the time to **slowly read through each chapter** and **complete each exercise** within the chapter before moving on. Also, you're invited to **make** the **exercises your own** and return to them to strengthen the concepts that resonate with you the most.

PART I

GENERATE INTERNAL PEACE

Nobody can bring you peace but yourself.

—RALPH WALDO EMERSON

For people who are high achievers accustomed to leaning heavily on their brains, it is challenging to understand the body's critical role in creating peace (and that the brain isn't enough). If you're the kind of person who is more comfortable *thinking* about your feelings than feeling them, or if that distinction escapes you, then I especially implore you to stick with me. Because believe it or not, the body is often the quickest route to transformation. (That knowledge surprised me too! But once I saw the results for both me and my clients, my resistance faded.)

In the pages that follow, we will explore ways to create a felt experience of peace from the inside out. You'll learn to harness the wisdom of your own unique and powerful body. You'll take control of the patterns that characterize your ever-shifting moods. And you'll become aware of your self-talk and fine-tune it to build yourself up, instead of beat yourself down. Prepare to strengthen your resilience, gain capacity to manage stress, and enjoy your calm.

Chapter One

LEVERAGE YOUR BODY'S WISDOM

The body is one of the most critical—and massively overlooked—tools to create deep and lasting internal change. Our body holds extraordinary wisdom. It sends us signals constantly about what we want and need and how we feel. We are born with the ability to access these systems, but over time, many of us disproportionately favor our intellect, ignoring and devaluing the signals from our body. I have been there (for decades!). Once we reach the point that we're screening out these signals, often we forget they were ever there to begin with. Instead of waiting until your body screams to get your attention through a chronic illness, health emergency, or other physical ailment, you can learn to listen *now*.

As an illustration, I once led a mindfulness workshop for a group of twenty or so stressed-out lawyers, a task for which I was uniquely well suited. I showed the group a simple breathing practice that involved slowly exhaling. As I looked across the room at the attendees dutifully breathing per my instructions, I saw furrowed brows, shoulders jacked up to ears, and backs hunched over. I felt a wave of empathy, remembering the way my own stomach clenched during law school when I would obsessively research cases. Here they were, trying to relax and immerse themselves in the here and now, but they had lost perspective on the amount of stress they were unconsciously retaining in their bodies. I explained to the workshop attendees that no amount of intentional breathing would work if their bodies remained constricted and constrained. I invited them to roll their shoulders down and back to create more space to breathe. Slowly, with repetition and intention, the group began to release their tension. They were smart, savvy, successful people, but their intellectual prowess failed them when it came to their physical awareness.

Similarly, my clients often come to me because their challenges are not intellectual ones. They find themselves stuck at a choice point in their work or personal lives. Or they have an existential yearning they can't articulate. Some feel like they are endlessly spinning their wheels. Still others are overwhelmed and tapped out but don't know what to do about it. They find that all their years of schooling, reading, scheduling, and life hacks—even therapy—are insufficient to fill the void they feel. These are the moments in our work together when we employ the body's wisdom to generate peace and insight.

Using the strategies outlined in this chapter, you will understand your body's signals again, so it becomes an ally for peace. You'll discover new ways to access your body's insights, and you'll learn to forge a more symbiotic relationship with your body, mind, heart, and spirit.

Learn to Communicate with Your Body

The first step in recruiting your body as an ally for peace is to open the lines of communication. I know this will sound strange, but you can speak to your body and ask it questions. You're probably thinking, *Wait, what?* But it's true: You can ask any hurt, ache, or tension in your body what it needs or what it's trying to tell you. Once you learn to listen, you'll find that your body will answer.

For example, one client complained of recurring headaches for which there was no medical cause. She had been wrestling with whether to leave a stressful job. We worked a great deal on patterns of thought like negative self-talk and routines that centered on well-being, but her headache persisted. One day, she came to a session with a headache. I led her through a practice of slowing down, breathing, and turning her attention inward. Then I invited her to ask the headache a direct question, "What are you trying to tell me?" Her headache answered very clearly: "You need rest and calm and quiet. Stop working so hard." That's a whole lot of insight from an ache!

As you regularly listen, you'll notice that your body sends signals all the time about what's working, what's not working, and what it needs from you. Some of the messages might be quite concrete, like: "You are hungry"; "You need to get up and move"; "This position is uncomfortable." And some may be more global, like: "You need a change"; "Your relationship is causing you suffering"; or "You're afraid to take on this challenge." This attunement takes practice, so be patient with yourself.

EXERCISE ❯ OPEN LINES OF COMMUNICATION

Sit down and take a deep breath in and out. Feel your feet on the floor. Let your body settle and relax. Bring your attention to your body. Your head and neck. Your arms and your legs. Your trunk and your abdomen. Your knees, ankles, and feet. As you scan each of these areas, notice if you have any aches, twinges, or discomfort. They may be obvious or quite subtle. Once you identify one, ask it, "What are you trying to tell me?" Notice any words, images, or intuitions that you sense.

To continue inviting this dialogue, you may try paying attention to the physical sensations that arise when you think about a challenge, a decision, or an opportunity. We often experience the physical sensations of fear, and its close cousin anxiety, most acutely. Fear shows up when there's any change in the status quo, and it tries hard to get our attention. You can allow the fear to be there and observe what else you sense. For example, behind that pit of fear in your stomach, is there also a surge of longing? Is that racing heart due to fear or excitement? Is that jiggling foot driven by restlessness or worry? You can cultivate the muscles of inquiry and discernment related to your body to generate insight.

EXERCISE › TAP INTO YOUR BODY'S INSIGHTS

Identify a challenge you want to resolve, but in which thinking your way to a solution has been unsuccessful. As you contemplate the challenge, notice the physical sensations that arise (e.g., a tightening in your chest, a rising in your belly, an anchoring in your feet, a hunching of your posture). When you notice these sensations, ask each of them, "What do you want me to know? What is my next course of action? What do I really want?"—or any other questions that pop into your mind. Then stay with the sensation and see if any insights come.

If other sensations appear, follow the same process. Often energy moves through the body as you gain new awareness. Your physical sensations are linked to one another, so allow organic sensations to arise.

Using exercises like these, my clients have gone from dumbfounded to astute when I ask how something feels in their body.

And they learn how to interpret their bodies' signals on their own. Because the body, mind, heart, and spirit are intertwined, regularly tuning in to their bodies' silent communication helps unlock greater emotional awareness.

With practice, you, too, can learn to access your own desires, confidence, and intuition (without interference from your logical brain—which carries all the woulds, shoulds, and can'ts that have been externally imposed on you by society and repeats them for you on a loop ad infinitum). Listening to signals from your body will help you develop a deeper and more nuanced understanding of your essential identity, because when you start to listen to what you really want, you begin to understand who you truly are.

The Three Power Tools of Perception

To set the stage for gaining greater body awareness, we need to detour into neuroscience (briefly—don't worry!). Each of us has three important systems through which we experience our body and our environment:

1. EXTEROCEPTION

This is your five senses—sight, sound, touch, taste, and smell. They help you take in the world and understand what's occurring in the present moment in the immediate context of your body.

2. PROPRIOCEPTION

This describes the ability to locate your physical self in space. Proprioception explains how you can touch your nose with your eyes closed (go ahead and try it), pick up a glass from a table, and maintain your balance while moving around.

3. INTEROCEPTION

This is the ability to experience sensations inside your body, such as butterflies in your gut, clenched muscles in your face, and heart palpitations.

Once you become conscious of these mechanisms, you'll find that they are power tools in your search for greater self-awareness. In day-to-day life, these systems operate outside of conscious awareness. If they didn't, we would walk around analyzing every sensation and movement, which would make higher-order thinking quite challenging, if not impossible. Through a process called embodied self-awareness, you can use your felt sense in the body to discover insights, to understand and shift your emotional state, to make choices, and to put enough distance between external stimuli and internal responses that you stop simply reacting and start choosing with intention.[1]

Move Your Body, Change Your Mood

Shifting your body posture and positioning can affect your felt sense of peace.[2] You've likely heard of Amy Cuddy, author of the controversial *New York Times* best-selling book *Presence: Bring Your Boldest Self to Your Biggest Challenges*, who writes about the power of the superhero pose to create more confidence. She explains that merely embodying this confident stance (hands on hips with feet shoulder-width apart) for even a few minutes can change the way you feel and perceive yourself in relationship to others. I have seen this principle borne out many times. When my clients talk about wanting more confidence, they automatically shift their bodies to stand more upright, solid, and firm, with their chests out—all without any prompting from me. Instead, it is clear they are unconsciously generating more confidence internally by moving their bodies into whatever configuration feels like confidence to them.

These principles don't just apply to confidence but to other emotions as well. For example, if you feel stuck but want to take action, try holding your body in a way that exhibits movement: lean forward, raise your eyebrows, shift your weight to the balls of your feet. If you want more joyfulness, embody the physical posture of joy, such as tilting your head up, smiling and having a lightness in your upper body. If this proves challenging, recall a moment when you experienced the desired emotion and allow your body to move naturally to express that feeling. Identify the distinctive body positions associated with that emotion, then practice reproducing those. It's like magic.

When I see my clients shift their body positioning (anything from a raised eyebrow to a slumped posture to a gesture they make unconsciously), I point it out to them and inquire about how they are feeling or what they are thinking. The body is a leading indicator of a shift. Over time, my clients learn to notice these physical changes themselves and use them to get curious about the emotions and thoughts that might be operating just beneath the surface. You can do this too and use it to your advantage to spur your own curiosity and self-awareness.

While your body's position affects your emotional experiences and thoughts, it is also the case that emotions evoke a physiological response. You are likely already aware of many of these. Fear is a drop in the stomach. Love is a soaring and swelling of the chest. Contentment is a settling of the belly, an ease in the shoulders. Your ability to understand your emotions is directly linked to how well you can feel and recognize their effects in your body.[3]

One client had difficulty being empathetic toward others when she was busy and stressed. Unfortunately, this skill was crucial for her as the leader of a large educational institution. As we dug in together, it was clear that she was unable to recognize the ways different emotions manifested in her body. "I guess I'm dead inside," she quipped. To help her shake this unconstructive (if dryly humorous) idea, I led her through an experience I've adapted from Amanda Blake, a thought leader in neuroscience and embodiment. I told her, "Hunch over, hang your head, and curl your stomach so your upper half is flopped over. Now try to feel enthusiastic." She looked at me like my mind had left the room.

"It's impossible," she said. "How can I feel enthusiastic this way?"

Her response was intuitive and correct: No, she couldn't possibly intellectualize her way to enthusiasm when her body was sending every signal possible that she was *not*. Down, defeated, humiliated, or deflated? Yes. But enthusiastic? Absolutely not.

"Now try this," I told her, moving on to the next phase of the exercise. "Sit up, allow your upper body to wiggle somewhat, grin, and bounce a bit in your seat. Now do you feel enthusiastic?" She smiled. *Yes.* This embodied—sometimes called *somatic*—experience helped her lock in the knowledge that physical postures and sensations directly affect thoughts and emotions and vice versa. Over time, she began paying greater attention to her physical sensations. She could identify stress more quickly and intervene with calming practices and lifestyle changes. This created space for empathy toward others (and herself).

EXERCISE ❯ EMBODY CALM[4]

Imagine you are stressed and don't want to be (you likely don't even have to imagine that hard). Notice how your shoulders creep up toward your ears, your head and neck push forward and down, your jaw sets tight, your butt feels clenched, or whichever is your unique, physical manifestation of stress.

continued

Now do the opposite of each of these physical gestures: Roll your shoulders down and back, adjust your neck and head upright, wiggle your jaw to loosen it, relax your butt. Notice the nuances of body positioning that are *your* unique physical signatures of peace. You will immediately feel calmer, even if not one thought changes. Of course, if you continue thinking fearful thoughts, your body will eventually slingshot back to a fearful posture. But using your body *and* your brain? That's a potent combination for lasting peace.

Here is a practical example of how using the brain-body connection can help overcome fear. One client was newly divorced and had just started dating. She felt fearful, tense, and avoidant when she considered the prospect of touching someone on a date. Instead, she wanted to feel excited, less guarded, and more intrigued. She believed that her avoidance was holding her back from moving on with her life. During our work together, I asked her to use a stool as a proxy for a man. As she stood facing the stool, imagining it was a man, her body naturally re-created the stressful sensations she experienced on a date: a rapid heart rate, a tense jaw, a lump in her throat, and a constricted stomach. Her whole body communicated panic. I asked her how she felt. "I am ready to flee," she said.

Instead of directly addressing that thought, we started with her body. I cued her, "Relax your shoulders down and back. Take two deep breaths." She tried it, looking looser and calmer as she did so. Her entire demeanor shifted. Once the breathing exercise was over, though, fear crept back in. There was an instantaneous change in her body language—she crossed her arms and tensed her jaw again. Once more, I invited her to breathe, soften her shoulders, and relax.

I asked, "How do you want to stand as you face him?"

"With my hands on my hips," she replied.

As she did so, some sass came in. She wiggled her hips, relaxed, and smiled. When her body loosened, so did her thoughts. In this calm, edgy body position, she was able to start accepting thoughts like, *I get to decide whether or how to touch* and *I'm curious to see what might happen between us here.* Using just her body, she was able to transform her emotions—and allow more positive thoughts to follow.

Merely telling yourself, "I am sassy" while walking around hunched over or constricted forces your mind and body to work at cross purposes. But reinforcing the thought *I am sassy* with equally confident body positioning communicates to your entire system that you are powerful, bold, edgy, and self-assured. Cool, right?

"

Intentionally synchronize your language with your physical posture (e.g., saying "I am strong" while standing grounded, firm, and upright). Then watch the exponential effects of your body and your brain being on the same team!

"

If you want to feel internal peace, hold your body in a way that conveys you are safe and well. Your shoulders are down and loose, your jaw soft, your feet grounded, your butt relaxed. Notice how calm you feel naturally without having to change your thinking. You are merely holding your body in alignment with the sense of peace you aim to enjoy.

People say, "Fake it 'til you make it," but I don't love that advice. It suggests we should act competent while simultaneously telling ourselves that competence is false. Instead, it's a vastly more effective approach to physically embody the posture and sensations that generate pride and confidence (or whatever emotion you wish to feel), and watch your brain follow your body's lead. For even greater impact, intentionally synchronize your language with your physical posture (e.g., saying "I am strong" while standing grounded, firm, and upright). Then watch the exponential effects of your body and your brain being on the same team!

Chill Out with Presence

It was an early morning. Yet, as soon as my client's face appeared on the screen for her coaching session, she launched into a rapid-fire update about everything going wrong in her life: conflict, struggle, kids, work. Her brown eyes blinked like a short-circuiting light, her chest rose and fell as if she were sprinting. I smiled and put my hand up, gently indicating for her to stop. Her speech skidded to a halt.

"Do you mind if we just breathe for a moment?" I asked.

"Yes, thank you," she answered breathlessly.

We took just a moment. "Place your feet on the floor and notice the solidity there," I prompted her. The muscles in her face unclenched. "Feel your back against the chair, supported." She straightened and then sank into her seat. "Let's take a few deep breaths here." Calm settled over us, and then a feeling of expansiveness. *Now* we could get to work. Once calmed, her nervous system could tolerate exploring what was really bothering her, and insights had space to emerge.

This example shows the power of presence: using body, breath, and senses to access calm. The simple act of breathing allowed her nervous system to shift. It moved from the sympathetic mode with its fight, flight, freeze, appease response where high-order thinking remains elusive, to the parasympathetic mode of rest and digest where imagination, creativity, and insights can bloom.

Your body is an anchor to the present moment. Physical sensations do not live in the past or the future—they exist only *now*.[5] If your back is aching, that felt sense of ache is right now, not yesterday or tomorrow. You perceive butterflies in your stomach because of the sensations of arousal at this moment. Once you understand the power of your presence in the current moment to access calm and tranquility, new possibilities emerge to manage challenging emotions. You are empowered to create sensations of peace *intentionally* at any moment you wish.

I am not suggesting you fully bypass negative emotions. Negative emotions contain important information for us: insight about ourselves and others, signals about our environment and context, and new information about patterns and ways of being in the world. By all means, experience the negative emotion and allow it to move through you. Hear its message and learn from it. However, many of us hang out in our negative emotions for way too long beyond the insights and information, and it sucks our energy and spirit.

Breaths That Unlock Calm

The breath is a natural way to sink into the present and self-regulate your emotions. It is always there for you. When you pay attention to your breath without making any conscious effort to change it, you will experience a calming and settling sensation. If you focus more deeply on your breath, you can tune out the outer world and its stressors. Your mind will quiet. Once you've removed these external influences, you can orient yourself to whatever you choose to focus on, instead of simply being reactive. The more you practice tuning in to your breath and tuning out the world around you, the quicker you can access calm, focus, and intention on purpose.

EXERCISE > JUST BREATHE

Set a timer for two minutes and simply notice your breathing. Your breathing happens all on its own. Pay attention to your breath, without changing anything. Don't hold or hasten your breath. Become aware of the natural rising and falling of your chest and stomach. This is a physiological miracle: Your body moves in intelligent synchrony to keep you alive. Afterward, check in to see if you feel any different than before you started. Are you more peaceful, centered, calm, or grounded?

EXERCISE > EXPAND YOUR BREATH

Whereas in the previous exercise you simply noticed your breath, you can also shift your breath to deliberately generate deeper tranquility. One technique for achieving this effect is the 4–7–8 Breath, which was created by an integrative physician named Dr. Andrew Weil. I have found that for people who have trouble settling their minds, the counting component of the 4–7–8 Breath gives their brains something to focus on.

Begin the breath by inhaling through the nose for a count of four, holding your breath for a count of seven, and exhaling for a count of eight. This breathing pattern yields a sense of calm, groundedness, and relaxation.

There are a few important notes here: The purpose of the count is to maintain a ratio where you exhale longer than you inhale. Everyone's breath pattern is different, so feel free to adapt the pace of the count so you feel comfortable with the length of the hold. Slow down the count or speed it up as needed.

continued

Before you begin inhaling, exhale the stale air already in your lungs with a sigh.

1. INHALE THROUGH YOUR NOSE FOR A COUNT OF FOUR

As you inhale, count in your head to four, keeping your tongue just behind your teeth with your jaw relaxed. Feel your belly expand.

2. HOLD YOUR BREATH FOR A COUNT OF SEVEN

This step presents the greatest challenge. Maintain your shoulders in the down and back position, sit up straight, and have a sense of calm as you hold the breath. You don't want to feel like you're struggling. Pay particular attention to your shoulders. If they are up near your ears and your chest is tight, you are conveying to your body that you are stressed. This counteracts the impact of the breathing. Adjust the count if you feel like this hold is too difficult, until it's comfortable.

3. EXHALE FOR A COUNT OF EIGHT

Make a whooshing sound as you exhale. You'll want to do several rounds of this breath to enjoy the full effect. I often do five rounds of the 4–7–8 Breath, keeping count on my fingers. The more you practice, the easier and more natural it will feel.

Body Awareness Scanning

Just as your breath can bind you to the present moment and focus your attention, the felt sense of your body can activate sensations of internal peace. As you go about your day, you're probably paying very little attention to what's happening inside your body (interoception) or noticing where your body is in space (proprioception). A technique called Body Scanning—a process by which you pay particular attention to the physical sensations of your body part by part—can help you connect with your body and the sense that all is well.

Safety and security are among our most basic human needs. When your brain spins about all the things that could go wrong in the future or rehashes some stressor that came up earlier in the day, you become consumed by it. Your body responds as if it's under attack right now: Your nervous system stands at high alert, sending your heart pounding, your skin sweating, your pupils dilating. A body scan anchors you to the fact that you are safe. Your brain focuses on deciphering the nuances of your actual current sensations, so your attention shifts to the current moment, instead of focusing on past or future worries. In a short time, your mind quiets, and your body calms.

EXERCISE 〉 PRESENCE YOUR BODY*

Go to my website, www.therootedrenegade.com/resources, for an audio version of this exercise.

Take a comfortable seat or lie down on the floor. Take your time moving through this exercise.

Begin at the top of your head. Gently nod your head *yes* and shake your head *no.* As you do this, notice the sensation of your skin as your head moves through space. Bring awareness to your neck muscles flexing and extending. Now allow your head to rest in stillness. Become aware of the stillness and what that feels like inside of you, and in all the space surrounding your head.

Bring awareness to your jaw. Is there tension or tightness there? Or is it resting in place?

Now move down to your neck. Feel the sensations inside your throat and on the skin of your neck. Is there stiffness there? Or lightness? Can you feel the air on your skin?

continued

Move on to your shoulders and chest. What sensations do you notice here? Weightiness, lightness, expansiveness?

Pay attention to your arms. Are they tense? Relaxed? Light? Do they seem impossibly long as you experience the sensations from your armpit all the way down to your fingers? Can you feel your individual fingers without touching them?

Now move back up your arms and down to your stomach and abdomen. What are you aware of as you attend to these parts of you? Is there any heat or coolness, softness, or constriction? See if you can feel the difference between the sensations outside of your body and within it. You might notice a fluttering in your belly or your clothes resting against your skin.

Move on to your bottom. Notice it supporting your body, all the way down to your thighs. Do they feel heavy, solid, agile? What are you aware of?

Now your knees. Are they bent or straight? Imagine the bones, ligaments, and tendons working in synchrony.

Down to the bottom of your legs, ankles, feet. What are you present to as you travel down your legs in your mind's eye? Can you feel the soles of your feet? Is there tingling or tightness? Groundedness?

Bring your attention to your toes. Can you feel your individual toes and how they exist together, side by side?

Take in the whole of your body from your head all the way to your toes. Feel the edges of your body against the air. Notice the space your body takes up. Feel the aliveness that's within you, the capacity for calm.

---

* Note: If you've experienced trauma specific to your body, please don't take on this exercise without the support of a therapist. For some of us, paying this much attention to our body is stressful and can elicit complex emotions (even if we haven't experienced trauma). If this applies to you, tread gently with yourself here. Instead of scanning your whole body, consider focusing extraordinary attention on a part of your body that feels safe. As an example, look at each finger on your hand. Notice how your fingers rest together. Take in your knuckles, fingernails, how the skin stretches gently across your bones. Connect with the power in your hands.

One Sense at a Time

Our brains constantly scan our environment, tuning in or tuning out information across our five senses. For example, before you read this sentence, you probably weren't aware of the feeling of your underwear (assuming you're wearing underwear!) against your skin or the sensation of your shirt on your back. But now that I've focused your attention, those sensations are available to you.

Tuning in to any *one* sense supports presence and calm by bringing awareness to the sensations at this singular moment in time. You can practice this focused attention with any of your five senses—vision, hearing, taste, smell, or touch—but hearing is often the most illuminating. As I tune in to the sounds around me, I hear the window fan, the clacking of computer keys, a car driving by, a plane overhead, my breath. Those are five distinct sounds I was oblivious to only moments ago. Bringing each of these sounds into my awareness, I notice that my surroundings appear as if I am seeing them anew. Focusing on my perception of the environment around me brings with it a slower heart rate, deeper breathing, and relaxed muscles. In just a few short moments, I have shifted to a state of peace. As with the breath exercises, the more you practice tuning in to your individual senses, the easier it will become to use your senses to generate tranquility and presence.

EXERCISE ❯ EVOKE YOUR SENSES

SOUND

Close your eyes and let your body settle into stillness. Allow the sounds of your environment to filter into your ears. As a sound comes into your ears, identify what you hear without rushing or forcing it. See if you notice the vibrations of each sound. Once you do, move on to the next sound

continued

you hear. Do this for one minute or so. When you finish, notice how your body feels as well as any shifts in your state of being.

SIGHT

Survey your space as a whole. Expand your vision outward so you aren't focused on one thing but rather on the gestalt of the space. Now choose an item that catches your eye and narrow your gaze upon it. Notice its features: textures, colors, shapes, lines, all of it, as if you're seeing it for the first time.

When you've fully examined this object, scan the room again, selecting another item and bringing it into focus. Again, take it in as if you're seeing it for the first time. See the details, the curves, the edges, the angles. Observe the hues, shades, and lightness.

When you are finished, notice how your body feels as well as any shifts in your state of being.

TOUCH

Hold your hands in front of you so they face each other, about half an inch apart. They are nearly touching. Notice the energy that exists between them. Now rub your hands together gently but vigorously for ten seconds. As you do this, feel the texture of your palms, the lines of your fingers, the smoothness or roughness of your skin.

Pause and hold your hands facing each other, about half an inch apart. Feel the heat you generated between them. There may even be an electric sensation on your palms, the aftereffects of movement. Move them closer together and farther apart and take in the distinct sensations.

When you are finished, notice how your body feels as well as any shifts in your state of being. If you wish to explore taste and smell, follow the same process of tuning inward and paying close attention to subtle sensations.

As you focus on each of your senses, your other senses likely fade into the background as if they don't exist. This is because your attention is singularly focused. Upon wrapping up each of these exercises, notice how you feel. Does your environment take on new complexity and nuance? This is what honing your awareness offers. Imagine if you did this a few times per day. When I practice this, I experience ready access to contentment, peace, awe, curiosity, and delight. My ability to create and imagine expands, too.

EXERCISE › REFLECT AND COMMIT

We've explored a range of high-impact strategies for cultivating internal peace using the body, from opening the lines of communication to using our posture, breath, and senses. Journal about the following:

- What have you discovered about your capacity to create peace through your body?
- What metaphor can you use to describe this new relationship with your body (e.g., soul mates, hand-and-glove, launch pad, home)?
- What commitment will you make to regularly integrate these practices into your life?

Schedule these practices into your calendar, create a note for yourself, write them in lipstick on the bathroom mirror—whatever works best for you.

Takeaways: Chapter One

✓ Learning to **communicate with your body** is essential for achieving deep, meaningful internal peace. Once you learn how to listen, your body can provide answers to the questions that confound your intellect.

✓ The three essential modes of perception are: **exteroception** (perception of the world around you using the five senses), **proprioception** (awareness of your body in space), and **interoception** (awareness of the sensations inside your body). These systems often operate outside of conscious awareness, but tuning in to them is a powerful tool for generating internal peace and promoting emotional self-regulation.

✓ Shifting your **body posture** to reflect the emotions you want to experience (e.g., confidence, calm, excitement) changes how you feel in real time, which can change your very thoughts. This methodology is more effective than the "fake it 'til you make it" approach, because the resulting emotions are *real*.

✓ Every felt sensation you experience in your body exists *now*, rather than in the past or future. In this way, **your body is an anchor to the present moment and to the fact that you are safe and well.** You can use this fact to your advantage and learn to focus your attention in order to self-regulate and generate more peace through **breathing exercises, body scanning,** and **tuning in to your senses one at time.**

Chapter Two

CULTIVATE PEACEFUL EMOTIONS

Several months ago, I received difficult news from the doctor. My biopsy showed that I had a growth on my thyroid with a 60 percent chance of being cancerous. There was only one option: remove my thyroid. I spent a few days crying and worrying and feeling frustrated by the limits of science. I let myself watch Netflix, nap, and then cry some more. I ate oyster crackers, then cried some more. I researched, reached out to friends, and—you guessed it—cried some more.

Finally, I was tired of merely distracting myself from despair and wanted to shift my mood and attitude. Importantly, I hadn't bypassed my negative emotions. I let them move through me fully first before choosing to change them. To begin the mood shift, I focused on gratitude: for doctors, ultrasounds, needles, biopsies, my insurance company, my husband; the list went on and on. Focusing on gratitude gave me the fortitude to make appointments and carry on with day-to-day life. And it prevented me from getting caught in a swirl of suffering. This is just one example of how focusing on gratitude has shown me personally that we can create patterns of thoughts and mood states to cultivate internal peace—on purpose.

Why Gratitude Matters

Gratitude is a gateway to presence, appreciation, connection, and a feeling of rightness in the world. When you tune in to gratitude, you are less likely to numb out of your emotional experiences and circumstances because you recognize that your fundamental needs are met. Gratitude also provides a solid footing from which to push against the edges of our comfort zone to lasso life.

There are many things in our lives that we simply consume without appreciation, from water to plastics to food. Take chocolate as an example. It's a delicious comfort for many of us. We can down a bag of chocolate easily, mindlessly eating it while binge-watching a TV series. Are we present to our gratitude for the chocolate in those moments? Probably not. We are barely tasting it.

There are gratitude meditations that signal the interconnectedness of humans and how miraculous each person's contribution is to bring you the object you are enjoying—including chocolate.[1] When you eat a piece of chocolate, you can use all your senses to fully enjoy it and be grateful for how that chocolate came to your mouth:

The farmers planted a seed and watched over it. The butterflies helped pollinate it. The water kept it growing. The sun shone on it. Farmers harvested it. People processed it and turned it into chocolate (opening pods, fermenting, drying, roasting, grinding, blending, molding). Someone packaged it. A truck driver put the chocolate on a truck and drove it to its destination. A clerk placed it on a shelf. A grocery cashier scanned it. You purchased it. Your hands unwrapped it. Your nose took in its scent. Your lips, tongue, and teeth worked together to eat it.

Notice how connecting with this gratitude affects you. It is incredible when you drill down to this level of appreciation for the little things that fill our lives. And this awareness conjures a fundamental contentment, which provides a home base to come back to and launch from again and again as we disrupt the status quo in our lives for the better.

The effect of gratitude has been studied and shown to facilitate our internal peace. Rick Hanson, a psychologist who studies and teaches about the integration of psychology, neuroscience, and contemplative practices, talks about letting positive, emotionally rich experiences like gratitude "really land." By this he means allowing them to "sink" into your body and intentionally staying with the emotional and physical experience for as long as you can.[2] You can allow your chest to warm and expand, your shoulders to soften, your nerves to settle. The sense of gratitude deepens, and the sensations reinforce themselves. This is different from jotting down a few things you are grateful for and moving on to checking your email. In that scenario, gratitude is simply an intellectual exercise, a check on your to-do list, not a deeply felt sense with its attendant system recalibration and calm.

Gratitude creates generative mood states in us. It's difficult to *simultaneously* feel gratitude and more challenging emotions like anger, fear, or worry. Rather, when you are fully in gratitude, you experience your heart opening, your tensions being relieved, a feeling of lightness. It can be a gateway to peace and other life-giving emotions (e.g., creativity, awe, delight, joy). You may even notice that gratitude inspires actions that better align with your purpose and legacy. With practice, gratitude can become the lens through which you view the world.

An experience for one client demonstrates the power of gratitude. She needed a walker and wanted to use it, but worried about how others might judge her. We sat in the worry, sadness, and fear, rather than bypassing those emotions. She wanted to shift her perspective, so I asked, "What's been beautiful about your hips? What have they given you?"

This gratitude frame opened a completely new thought process about the history of her family that lived in her degenerating hips. Dancing, fun, adventure in her life, and memories she relished were all made possible by her hips. Her face lit up as she wiggled and swayed, remembering the joy of dancing in her younger days. "If someone had told me that these experiences would make my hips decline faster, I wouldn't have traded them," she said with a laugh.

Seeing her joyfully shift in her seat and yearn to fully express what her body had within, I challenged her to try chair belly dancing. She sought sexiness, movement, and sensuality. Gratitude opened a portal to all that richness. The energy of her gratitude was completely different from how she had started. And it planted the seed for a different relationship with her whole body.

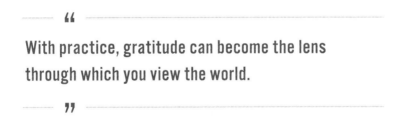

With practice, gratitude can become the lens through which you view the world.

Gratitude for Your Body

Why is the relationship between gratitude and the body so important? Your body takes you to the edge of your comfort zone and beyond. Your body is not just a traveling vessel for your brain; it's your access point to full-out living, composed of sensory experience, deep levels of knowing that you experience in your gut and your bones, emotional experience, access to the present moment, and so much more. However, if you are at war with your body, continually assaulting it with hard words and actions, generating internal peace is challenging.

With my clients who want to change their inner monologue about their bodies or who deal with frustrating chronic health concerns, our work often includes them connecting with gratitude for their bodies. Some clients experience understandable resistance to this gratitude. "There's nothing I'm grateful for. My body is a mess," one client said, pointing out every issue she was facing. Yes, those feelings of frustration, disappointment, and anger are there. It's important to give them time and space to be felt and empathized with by others. And when my clients have metabolized those feelings and are ready to try something different, we shift to gratitude.

The starting point for gratitude can be an eyebrow, an elbow, a patch of skin, a finger, an organ that is functioning exceptionally. Even in the direst physical conditions, there are *millions* of processes, cells, neurons, organs, hormones, and chemicals that are working well, but we can forget this amid our suffering.

Coming up, you will find a powerful body gratitude practice, which is a twist on the Body Scan exercise. Ready to start rewiring your understanding of the wisdom and magnificence of your body? If you experience many challenging thoughts and feelings related to your body, instead of going through the whole exercise, start by focusing on a small part of your body that you believe works well (think: your pinkie, elbow, belly button, ear, etc.).

This practice can support you to create a different relationship with your mind, heart, and body, in service of generating the internal felt sense of peace. Trust that you will get what you need from this process.

EXERCISE ⟩ GENERATE BODY GRATITUDE*

Go to my website, www.therootedrenegade.com/resources, for an audio version of this exercise.

Let the questions and musings contained in this script wash over you instead of trying to answer them explicitly. You will have an opportunity to journal afterward.

Take a seat or lie down, whichever is most comfortable for you. Feel your body supported, still, and held. Take a deep breath in through your nose, all the way to your belly. Exhale, relaxing and releasing. Again, inhale through your nose all the way to your belly and out, letting go.

Start at the top of your head. Bring awareness to your head, your hair, your skull that protects your brain. This beautiful head of yours contains a universe of potential within it. Your brain helps you breathe, see, think, connect, read, write—all the many tasks throughout your day and life. How has your mind supported you? What are you grateful to your mind for? Which environments support it? What does your mind need to thrive?

Moving to your face. Your eyes that take in the lovely colors of the world around you, that see the smiles of your loved ones. Your nose that smells the scent of home or brings you the appetizing aromas of your favorite dinner. Your lips that kiss and move with each letter you speak effortlessly. This lovely face is yours.

Down to your chest, your heart. Your breath. The ceaseless beating of your heart that speeds up and slows down whenever you need. What is your heart carrying that you're ready to let go of? What does your heart need to work its best? How do you want to care lovingly for your heart and your lungs? This incredible partnership carries you through your whole life.

continued

Your back with its vertebrae and spinal column keeps you upright, bending, seated, standing, carrying. It's the fortitude in you. What does your back want you to know about the strength that resides in you?

Down to your legs, knees, feet, and toes. These parts with their joints, ligaments, tendons, and bones help you move through the world, seeing new sights, standing upright feeling the ground beneath you. What are you called to appreciate about how you move?

Now take in your whole body from your head to your individual toes. Feel the essence that is you in your head, your heart, your arms, your legs, your feet. You are in your whole self. There's no disconnection or divide. You are a seamless, whole, beautiful body. Your spirit moves through all of you.

You have been gifted this incredible body. It will accompany you for your whole life. Notice any inklings of calm, surrender, and appreciation. Journal your observations.

---

* Note: If you've experienced trauma specific to your body, please don't take on this exercise without the support of a therapist.

Mind Your Mood

Many of us are familiar with the power of the imagination to rehearse a task and enhance performance, like elite athletes who picture a jump shot or a complicated gymnastics routine.[3] Your imagination is also a powerful tool to impact your mood. By purposefully imagining the people, places, ideas, and experiences that generate the feelings you want to have, you create those feelings within yourself. The next exercise demonstrates how to begin.

EXERCISE ⟩ HARNESS YOUR IMAGINATION

Consider a place where you feel safe and calm. It might be your living room couch, your bed, a mountaintop, a lake, or a beach. Wherever it is, allow yourself to imagine being there. Everything is just as it needs to be. Notice the emotions and sensations that arise, such as spaciousness, calm, connection, safety. Which emotions do you notice? What are the physical imprints of these feelings? Tune in to your chest, your belly, your neck, your face.

Notice how quickly you were able to generate these calming emotions simply using your imagination. You can use this practice to create peace whenever you wish: before a stressful meeting, lying in bed, or walking down the street.

The body is a gateway to understanding your emotions. The body often has a micro-reaction before you have a conscious thought. Unfortunately, many of us pay so little attention that we fail to notice these reactions. Have you ever experienced a sense of anxiety, but you weren't aware of its cause? Have you ever had the experience of seeing someone and your heart flutters? Or you've had a gut sense that something was wrong, but you couldn't articulate it? These are examples of the body being out ahead of your thoughts. Your body is like a tuning fork, but you need to learn how to listen to and interpret it.

You can train yourself to notice the way different emotions feel physically by slowing down, turning inward, and deciding what you want to make of them. Once you know what different emotions feel like, you can re-create these sensations and emotions purposefully.

EXERCISE > IDENTIFY YOUR EMOTIONS' PHYSICAL IMPRINTS[4]

Think of someone you love deeply and unconditionally. Picture them and let yourself sink into the sensations of unconditional love. What's happening in your chest? Perhaps it warms or expands. Maybe you find your body leaning forward. What do you notice in your stomach? How about your jaw and face?

Now think of something you long for, something you so wish would come to pass. Imagine that achievement, possession, relationship, or experience. Whatever it is, let yourself long for it. Allow the longing to expand in you. What sensations do you notice? Tune in to your chest, your stomach, and your shoulders. Is there an up and outward reaching in your chest and stomach? Are your shoulders back? Does your body feel light? Do you experience heat or expansiveness in your belly?

Repeat this process of imagining an idea, an item or possession, a place, a person, or an experience that evokes in you the emotions in the following list. Slow *way* down here and tune in to *each* of these emotions. Try not to overthink this. Go with the first image, idea, or person that comes to mind when you read the word. Your body will reveal the physical imprint of these different mood states, if you let it.

- Tranquility
- Respect
- Contentment
- Awe
- Curiosity

- Abundance
- Speaking truth
- Playfulness/joy
- Humor
- Calm

When you want to create these emotions on purpose, call up these physical sensations using the anchor of an idea, an item or possession, a person, a place, or an experience. Then grow these sensations: make them more intense, deeper, and expansive.[5] If you're having a hard time with this process, use a vivid memory—recall a moment when you felt this helpful emotion intensely. Picture the scene as concretely as you can, in lots of detail, while being present to the felt senses of the emotions.

How can you use this competency? Let's say I'm bored and plodding through my work tasks. If I want to feel playful, I can recall a moment when I felt that way: playing fetch with my dog and his elephant toy. I was sitting on the ground, romping around, and eliciting happy barks. My body was bouncy, my feet were light, and my face beamed. Inside of me was a vibrating sensation, a rising of my belly, a feeling of explosive energy. I feel all of that now as I imagine that moment. And I can grow these sensations by bringing my attention to them. Now I can use this playful mood as I go about my work.

As you practice, summoning the emotions will become more natural. You are simply doing on purpose what your body does effortlessly without your awareness—and, in turn, guiding your emotional experience.

Abundance Is the Antidote to Scarcity

It is difficult to feel calm and resourceful in the face of scarcity. Rather, scarcity breeds panic, a singular focus on acquisition, a tendency to hoard, and so on. All of this is contrary to contentment and tranquility. When I left my job to stay home with our baby, money was tight. We had sold our home, at a loss, so that my husband wouldn't have to commute and be away from our family. Grocery trips were a series of difficult choices. And yet, when I focused on my capacity for creation, I could consider the limitations as a game. I relished beets with the leaves on—two nights of veggies! I repurposed leftovers: Chicken breasts morphed from salad toppings to quesadillas to soup. By shifting my mindset toward gratitude for the versatility of options in the store and for my own creativity, I fostered feelings of abundance where a scarcity mindset had been my default reaction.

At the time of writing, layoffs and inflation are pervasive. The global economic scales feel tenuous. This understandably can trigger concerns over competition for resources, fears of inadequacy, and anxiety about financial instability. These feelings are valid, and they are wired into our neurobiology. If we didn't have these fears baked in, we'd be hanging on the savannah chatting it up while our tribe was out of food. Not a great recipe for species survival!

In his book *The Abundance Project: 40 Days to More Wealth, Health, Love, and Happiness*,[6] Derek Rydall talks about experiencing a sense of abundance that is separate from circumstances. He says the feelings of being safe, of having what we need, of peace and freedom are within us—no Porsche necessary.

Hedonic adaptation is real: We acclimate to our circumstances, so we end up wanting more. When you get a new car, it feels amazing for the first couple of months as you drive, enjoying how the seats feel and relishing the features. Six months or a year goes by, though, and somehow it has lost its luster. That spurs a hedonic treadmill for more, better, different. Even lottery winners acclimate to their winnings and often return to their baseline happiness levels within a year.[7] Accordingly, even when we have plenty, it can feel like not enough. The need for acquisition drowns out contentment.

There are two ways to generate the baseline feeling of abundance:

1. BODY-BASED APPROACH

Know what abundance feels like in your body and re-create those sensations.

2. THOUGHT-BASED APPROACH

Truly understand your extensive capacity to create and generate abundance—using your skills, talents, interests, and experiences.

You can master either or both approaches with persistence and practice.

EXERCISE > CREATE FEELINGS OF ABUNDANCE[8]

Imagine that you've just received a beautiful gift you love. It's exactly what you wanted. You may feel seen, appreciated, loved, fortunate, safe, and/or calm. Notice:

- What emotions are present?
- How do you feel in your body? Perhaps your chest expands, lightens, and lifts. Maybe a feeling of calm washes over your shoulders and down your entire body. Perhaps your feet feel anchored and grounded. You may notice a buzzing on the surface of your arms or legs.

Pay attention to all the sensations in your body. You are building the felt-sense memory of abundance so you can create these feelings on purpose when it serves you.

The next time you want to feel peace and calm, but scarcity creeps in, call up the physical sensations you identified previously and grow them: make them more intense, deeper, more expansive. And if this is too challenging, allow your mind to focus on something you feel abundant about: air, water, sunshine, love, brilliance. Then notice the physical sensations and emotions that arise from thinking about that beautiful abundance. Practice generates ease.

The second way to generate abundance is through your thoughts. This is an invitation to get specific and clear on your extraordinary capacity to create. If you understood the vast resources within you, it would be easier to repel scarcity thinking and generate greater calm.

Consider the raw materials you can create from economically: knowledge, creativity, physical skills, connections, and talents. All of that is within you, which is mind-boggling. For example, my husband is skilled at computer programming, IT, management, fixing things around the house, and getting his dad buddies to connect. He could leverage these skills into a mentoring position, a handyperson business, a website that connects dads socially, and so on. As another example, our contractor is adept at budgeting, managing people, carpentry, motivating others, and organization. He could use these skills to create his own business managing vacation homes, organizing large-scale projects of any sort, and training others how to motivate and retain talent. Consider, there are over thirty-three million small businesses in the US; all those people created something from nothing, using their diverse skill sets to generate abundance for themselves, their families, and their communities.[9]

Most of my clients who are considering a career change are overwhelmed by the options, not underwhelmed by limitations, once they recognize how vast their skill set is. Learning to identify and leverage these skills can generate feelings of possibility and abundance. I invite you to generate a list of your skills, talents, experiences, things you enjoy doing, and the like, and see how long you can make it!

In some ways, this process is circular: As you become present to this source of creation and capacity, you will likely notice the body-based sensations of abundance that you explored in the previous exercise. Pretty cool, right? That means you have two access points—your body and your thoughts—and they are mutually reinforcing.

Master Energetic Release

Another way to generate peaceful emotions is to allow the fiery emotions to move through you, instead of stifling them. Many of us who have been socialized as women and other marginalized identities have internalized sexism, racism, homophobia, transphobia, and the like. This manifests as self-editing, feeling responsible for others' emotions, staying small, honoring others' expectations over our own, or wrestling with self-doubt. We need to learn how to safely discharge our silenced emotions.

Many people think that to experience calm you need more relaxing activities like massage, meditation, yoga, and the like (which you probably do). But you often don't have a release for the energetic intensity you experience and internalize daily. Instead, you may get backaches, stomachaches, muscle tension, headaches, and shrunken posture. It's no surprise that inflammation and other physical manifestations take root.

Internal peace is elusive when we are sitting with stifled words, energy, or emotions. Think of it as sludge gunking up the machinery of peace. In this case, an energetic release can help. Yelling words or sounds like *Ahhhhh! Rahhhhh! Rrrrr!* or *Uhhhhh!* helps energy leave the body.[10] This practice should not be directed at a person, of course, but into a pillow, a forest, underwater, or outside. The more guttural the sounds, the better. Breathe all the way into your belly, then release again and again until you feel empty of obstructions.

When I was giving birth to my youngest child, my doctor came running upon hearing these types of guttural noises emanating from my room. "I heard the sound of a mama about to have her baby," she said. These noises came through me but not from me. They were as involuntary as the contractions of my uterus. My body knew how to move the incredible energy through me and give me strength and release at the same time.

I invite you to channel your primitivity: Release the sounds that well up within you, as if there's an open channel from deep in your body all the way to your mouth. By all means, yell, groan, screech, bellow! And if that's hard to get behind, consider screaming curses into the wind (this was particularly helpful to me during the low moments of the early pandemic). This type of ferocious release has the side effect of counteracting social messages about being too much, too loud, or not important—bonus!

Another means of emotional release and reset is to acknowledge your emotions and allow them to move all the way through you. Many of us have a limited emotional vocabulary: love, joy, fear, anger, sadness, and the like. However, there are many nuances that describe a wider range of emotions. As an example, Brené Brown covers eighty-seven different emotions in her book *Atlas of the Heart*.[11] When you name the emotion you are feeling *specifically*—a concept called emotional granularity, coined by researcher Lisa Feldman Barrett—your system responds positively. And research shows that gaining more competency at this practice is associated with greater well-being.[12]

You've likely had the experience of talking to a friend or partner, and you can't quite put your finger on how you feel. When the other person offers up a suggested label for the emotion you're trying to express and they nail it, you feel seen, heard, and validated. You can do that for yourself by identifying how you feel *specifically*. Consider the nuances of jealous or enraged or resentful versus the general emotion, anger. Or the distinctions of lonely or regretful or hopeless versus the general emotion, sad. On my website you'll find links to emotion wheels, a helpful tool to build your emotion vocabulary (www.therootedrenegade.com/resources).

To metabolize and release emotions, you can practice allowing and being with sidelined emotions that dwell within you: anger, frustration, lust, jealousy, passion, and fear. Emotions are like waves. They have an intelligent rise, crest, and fall, but you interrupt this cycle when you squash them down. Give your emotions time and space to crescendo, then release. And trust that the release and relief will come.

When I hold space for a client to be in their emotions, I'm struck that it often takes only a few minutes for the emotion to move through them. I witness the transformation as the constriction loosens in their shoulders, throat, and posture, and their face reflects relief. We all know the effect of a good cry: solace, satisfaction, the sense that an emotional junk drawer has been emptied. The tranquility awaiting on the other side of our challenging emotions is wired into us. Yet, many of us spend a lifetime at great cost avoiding what would otherwise be a short while in the throes of it.

“

Give your emotions time and space to crescendo, then release. And trust that the release and relief will come.

”

You may require an expulsive activity to allow these emotions to move through you like a rage walk (that's me with aggressive pumping arms and stomping feet), or jumping jacks, or a run. Or you may need something gentler. You can set yourself up in a comfortable, safe space and create a ritual that you enjoy, like pouring yourself a cup of tea, lighting a candle, sitting in a special place in your home, or walking in nature. Make it yours. Finally, you can shake your arms, your hands, your whole body, and let the energy move through you. It's wildly satisfying.

Amanda Blake, a somatic coach and neuroscientist, notes that after a near-death chase with a predator, a gazelle lies on the ground and shakes until they calm down and release the energy of that stressful event. We don't normally allow ourselves this type of release that's incredibly natural and necessary. Instead, that stress soaks back into us and seeds trouble.

I have seen this clearly in my own life. One of my children had a sensory processing disorder when they were younger. They were often overcome by sensory inputs. Their natural response was to shake their arms and their head to release the feelings of overwhelm and reset their system. After a minute or so, they were regulated. Their system knew intuitively what they needed.

Your system knows what you need, too. It's just that your socialization dampens your self-knowledge in this domain. Fundamentally, if you regularly practice releasing your emotions in ways that resonate for you, it will be easier to clear a path for internal peace.

EXERCISE > CLEAR ENERGETIC CRUD

Make a list of things you're holding inside: things unsaid, emotions underexpressed, words you've whispered when you wanted to scream them, wounds unacknowledged. Make a sound for each item that expresses what you've been holding back. *Let it rip!* Crescendo and then soften once you're empty. Depending upon the size of your list, this may take awhile. Allow yourself the time and space to honor your full list. Engaging in soothing self-care afterward can be helpful to restore equilibrium.

The afterglow that comes from emptying that which has been stifled is magical. Notice how your muscles, bones, nerves, and skin settle into a new spaciousness. This is fertile ground for internal peace.

Identify Peace-Busting Behavioral Patterns

Are you entitled to internal peace even if you get angry easily; yell, snap, or are sarcastic with people; binge eat, drink, or scroll? Yup! But it doesn't feel great to regularly engage in these behaviors. Never fear: You can use your body to shift these destructive emotional patterns that erode your peace and cause you strife.

One client was stuck in a stubborn pattern of yelling at her child, which she desperately wanted to change but didn't know how. Her child was very physical and often didn't comply with her directions to stop climbing on furniture and being destructive around the house. My client would ask the little girl to stop; the child wouldn't. My client would get frustrated and yell. Then my client would feel guilty about yelling, think she was being a bad mom, and pledge not to do it again. But the cycle eventually repeated itself. She didn't see a way to change the dynamic and felt destined to a difficult life at home—and a challenging inner monologue of self-recrimination.

To understand emotion-based patterns like this, you need to look at what's happening in your body. Your physical sensations are like the first orange streaks of a sunrise. They flash before you have the language or the thoughts to describe them. And you likely miss these early signs, repeatedly. To counteract that, you can begin to observe your patterns as if in slow motion and notice each microstep. Then you can determine ways to intervene and break patterns that don't serve you.

When you slow way down, you become aware of the *physical sensations that precede a pattern*. I call these *physical tells*. In poker, a tell is a signal you give off that other players can interpret—or read—to mean you have a good hand, poor hand, or are going to make a particular move. Similarly, in real life, we can learn to read our physical tells to predict various emotions, thoughts, or actions.

When my client and I examined the pattern together, we saw that many smaller steps in rapid succession led up to an emotional blowout. We slowed down to consider each step. We realized her physical tells at the outset: Her cheeks flushed and her heart raced. A negative thought followed: *My kiddo is so difficult and always will be.* Afterward came the emotions of frustration, sadness, and grief. And ultimately, yelling.

> **"**
>
> **Slowing down and reflecting on your patterns outside of the moment enables you to notice what's happening in order to shift it.**
>
> **"**

To change this pattern, she needed to intervene early in this cycle when her cheeks first felt flushed. To calm down, I encouraged her to focus on the sensations she felt in her body in the *present*. I suggested she feel her feet on the floor and take a calming breath, followed by speaking to herself reassuringly: "This is just one moment"; or "She's a little girl who's having a hard time"; or "I'm a good mom and can manage this."

These types of patterns happen in seconds, almost automatically. Slowing down and reflecting on your patterns outside of the moment enables you to notice what's happening in order to shift it. You are *not* destined to repeat your peace-busting patterns! You *can* interrupt them and practice something different.

EXERCISE ❯ FIND YOUR TELLS

Consider a pattern that you want to change. It might be snapping at a partner, procrastinating on an important task, resisting setting boundaries with friends or family, and so on. Pick something that occurs often in your life.

Imagine the scene happening in your mind, as if you're watching a movie about the pattern. What happens first? Often, what we *think* happens first is actually the third or fourth step. Try to rewind in your mind's eye and think about what preceded that "first step." Notice the first physical sensation you experienced during the interaction. It might be a lump in your throat, a flush of your cheeks, a rapid heartbeat, heaviness in your body, or a sinking of your posture.

Is there a thought that accompanies these sensations? Some examples might be:

Here we go again!

Why can't I get this right?

You always do this!

Why am I stuck in this situation?

What's wrong with you?

Identify whether these thoughts are directed at you or someone else. If they are directed at someone else, remind yourself that you can only change *your* thoughts, reactions, and actions. The other person is responsible for themselves.

Notice if you are projecting into the future (e.g., *My kid is going to become a criminal* or *My partner and I will fight about this forever*) or foisting the past into the present (e.g., *You always/never, etc.*). Doing this will raise the temperature on all your emotions. Of course, you feel what you feel. Let yourself do that, but if you want to change your own reactions, dialing down the temperature will help.

Shift Peace-Busting Behavioral Patterns

Now that you have identified these patterns, it's time to start changing them. Here are four steps for interrupting unhelpful emotional patterns and creating more constructive ones instead:

1. SOOTHE THE BODY

To bring calm to your body, use the breathing exercises we discussed earlier on page 27 or the presence-enhancing practices in subsections Body Awareness Scanning and One Sense at a Time on pages 28–33.

2. IDENTIFY THE THOUGHTS, THEN NARROW THEM

Examine the situation and identify which thoughts are present. Writing them down can help you to view them more objectively. If you're projecting into the future or bringing up the past, shift your focus to what's here and now. If you're beating yourself up, stop, and attempt self-compassion instead (reference the self-talk and self-compassion discussions in Chapter Three on page 61, Chapter Six on page 101, and Chapter Seven on page 148 for helpful hints). If you're stuck in absolute or all-or-nothing thinking, remember that while your brain loves that, it's seldom based on the nuance of the situation.

Instead of Thinking	Try
They always leave their socks on the floor.	I'm frustrated by the socks on the floor today.
We will never work out this issue.	We'll have a conversation about this now.
I can't ever get things done on time.	I haven't figured out a strategy for this project yet.

3. COMMIT TO THINKING THOUGHTS THAT WILL SERVE YOU

Ask yourself, "What thought will serve me to create the feelings I want to have?" Consider choosing thoughts that center your autonomy, power, and self-compassion. Your brain is incredibly malleable. Once you are aware of your thoughts and recognize that your thoughts contribute to how you feel, you can choose to deliberately shift them.

Instead of Thinking	Try
She/he/they won't unload the dishwasher.	I'm in charge of my own actions and reactions (notice the personal responsibility).
I'm a terrible mom.	I messed up; I'm human (notice the self-compassion).
I'm not smart enough to do this job.	I have accomplished a lot; I'll figure out what I need to know (notice the self-compassion and confidence).

4. DECIDE ON ACTIONS YOU WILL TAKE TO INTERRUPT AND SHIFT THE PATTERN

Every time your early physical tells happen, or you find yourself in the same circumstance, what will you commit to doing differently? For example: calming your body, using reassuring thoughts, accessing your compassion for the other person, changing your setting by going outside, or moving your body in a way that feels good to you. When you see the pattern starting, uttering an "OOPS!" internally or externally and/or using a gesture like putting your hand up or clasping your hands together can help. You are noticing, catching yourself, and then choosing something different.

Remember, making the shift requires lots of practice. You are literally rewiring your brain to create more peace for yourself (and those around you). Instead of feeling only disappointed, rejoice when the unhelpful pattern shows up—it means more opportunities to practice! If you're irritated at me right now, I get it. My clients feel that way, too, when I say this.

Telling on Yourself to Develop More Peaceful Habits

We have many mindless habits that make us feel crappy, but we are often unaware of them in the moment. For example, I become intensely focused on cleaning my kitchen when I need to edit writing (ahem, including this book). The dishes call me. The crumbs long to be swept up. The coffee machine needs a scrubbing. When I finally recognize that I'm scrubbing instead of editing, that's the moment I have power. I say to myself, "I'm cleaning because I am nervous about editing my work. I'm procrastinating." Immediately, my entire body settles, as if I've released a secret that I was keeping from myself. I feel liberation and calm simply in naming the behavior. I am empowered to continue making the same choice and clean joyfully or to choose something different—but the heat or intensity of my behavior dissipates. In its place is *intention*.

You can generalize the technique of Telling on Yourself to many different contexts by calling out the behavioral pattern explicitly. The key is to do so without judgment. You're merely stating the facts. Extra points if you can do it with self-compassion, but for many of us, neutral is a good place to start.

What telling on yourself looks like:

- I'm getting a snack because I'm bored, not hungry.
- I'm procrastinating because I'm scared that I may fail.
- I'm being hard on myself intentionally because I think it helps.

- I'm avoiding calling my friend because I don't want to have an uncomfortable conversation.

EXERCISE ⟩ BUST A HABIT

Choose a habit that's not serving you (e.g., going to bed late, binge-watching TV, procrastination). Practice telling on yourself each time you do the habit. You're simply naming the motivation behind the behavior, *not* attempting to change the behavior. But as you practice, notice if there are any shifts in the intensity or frequency of the habit.[13]

Takeaways: Chapter Two

✓ You can **purposefully create patterns** of thought that cultivate an internal sense of peace.

✓ **Gratitude is a powerful tool** that can help you practice presence, appreciation, and connection, and tap into a feeling of rightness in the world. Gratitude is a gateway to peace and other life-giving emotions. Consciously practicing gratitude can help **rewire your relationship to the power and wisdom of your body,** allowing you to access alignment, integration, and peace.

✓ You can **use your thoughts and knowledge of how emotions feel in you to create any emotion you wish.** Use your imagination to seed peaceful thoughts that will begin to come more naturally over time. **Practice generates ease!**

✓ **Scarcity and abundance can be mindsets you adopt regardless of your external circumstances.** It is possible both to fear scarcity when you have plenty and to feel abundant when you have very little. The power is yours to choose which mindset you use to move through the challenges and obstacles that you face.

✓ There are two ways to create the baseline feeling that **we have everything we need and have limitless possibility** to create resources for ourselves:

1. BODY-BASED APPROACH

Know what **abundance feels like in your body** and **re-create those sensations.**

2. THOUGHT-BASED APPROACH

Truly understand your **extensive capacity to create and generate financially** and **otherwise**—using your skills, talents, interests, and experiences.

✓ **Energetic release** is a deeply cathartic way of regulating emotions and releasing tension. Taking a rage walk, shaking your body, and releasing intense sounds from within are a few practices that discharge emotions.

✓ **Naming emotions specifically** and allowing them to move through you like a wave can help to metabolize and release emotions.

✓ You can **identify the beginning of destructive emotional cycles by the physical symptoms they conjure.** The more attuned you are to your body's tells, the more able you will be to recognize the signs of an unhelpful emotional cycle starting up. Once you've recognized the pattern, you can practice intervening at an early stage to shift these emotional patterns toward more peaceful habits.

✓ There are **four steps for interrupting unhelpful emotional patterns** and creating more constructive ones instead:

1. Soothe **your body.**

2. Identify and narrow **your thoughts.**

3. **Commit to thinking** thoughts that will serve you.

4. Decide what actions you will take to **shift this pattern.**

✓ To **shift mindless habits** that feel crappy, start by **gently telling on yourself.**

Chapter Three

HARNESS SELF-TALK

"What does your self-talk sound like?" I asked my client.

"You mean the voice in my head?" she asked.

"Yes, the voice that travels with you wherever you go. It might be encouraging and motivating, or harsh and critical, or have other qualities depending upon what you're doing and how you're feeling."

"Well, that's easy because it's the same words all the time. 'You don't know what you're talking about. Who do you think you are? Everyone is going to find out that you're an idiot. You tricked them into getting this job. Eventually you'll fail; it's just a matter of time.'"

I noticed how blasé my client appeared rattling off these offenses, as familiar as the bread and eggs on a grocery list. We have more work to do when we aren't upset about our horrid self-talk because it feels so normal. Like most things, identifying the issue is the first powerful action. Most of us struggle with negative self-talk. Transforming this aspect of our inner world unlocks so much possibility.

Negative self-talk has pernicious effects in all aspects of our lives. You may self-limit your potential by avoiding jobs that stretch you because you've told yourself that you're not capable. Perhaps you stay in a relationship because of the self-deception that this is the best you deserve. You may even undermine your fulfillment and satisfaction by minimizing your accomplishments and gifts. Finally, you become so depleted from trying to build yourself up from the self-talk that cuts you down that you simply give up: play small, avoid your potential, forget your dreams. But it doesn't have to be that way. There are many approaches to work on this issue, so read on!

Your Words Matter

You speak more to yourself than to anyone else. Your inner monologue can motivate you or bring you to your knees. Perhaps you believe that beating yourself up internally is the key to your success because it motivated you through challenging training and career trajectories. *Wrong!* Have you ever worked on a difficult task while someone yells at you? Most of us flounder and suffer. Even if verbally abusive self-talk *momentarily* improves your focus, forget about a peaceful and joyful existence under this internal tyranny. Rather, it comes at a cost of physical and emotional suffering. This may manifest as not sleeping, not eating, overworking, getting sick, pushing yourself to your absolute limits, being unable to say no, being constantly on edge and anxious, and so much more.

Isn't it horrendous? You'd never speak this way to someone you care about or want them to suffer in this way. Yet, you end up abusing the person you should care about most: yourself.

Four Steps to Improve Negative Self-Talk

1. BE AWARE

When we become aware of our self-talk, most of us notice it is nearly nonstop and is almost always negative. Some physical manifestation of stress usually follows negative self-talk: a rapid heartbeat, sweating, or a roiling stomach. Think of a negative phrase you often say to yourself, and pay close attention to the physical sensations. Now imagine this assault happening to your body all day long. As you go about your week, notice when you are speaking to yourself harshly. Try not to judge; simply notice. If it feels shocking initially, reassure yourself that understanding the scale and impact of your internal negativity can catalyze more motivation to change.

2. NOTICE THE NEED

Most of our fundamental unconscious needs boil down to safety/security/control, love/belonging/approval, and competence/self-actualization/meaning/feeling our place in the world.[1] When negative self-talk appears, ask yourself: "Which fundamental need is in jeopardy underneath my words?" For example, "I am a sucky writer. I'll never finish this, and even if I do, everyone will hate it." What you're really worried about is security (perhaps of your job, position, title), approval by others (readers, your boss, your colleagues), and self-actualization (doing high-quality work and carrying out your purpose). This—ahem—is a familiar example to me. Which needs underlie your most common negative self-talk?

If your negative self-talk focuses around your relationships, it might sound like, "No one likes me. Why would they? I'm so different from everyone else." What underpins those specific concerns is belonging: "Can I accept myself, and will others accept me? Will I be loved?"

When your negative self-talk runs amok, one of these needs is likely feeling threatened. You can respond by intentionally focusing your self-talk to address this compelling underlying need.

3. INTENTIONALLY REFRAME

Building upon this awareness, you can consciously reframe your negative self-talk to create a peaceful, loving, internal presence. The goal is for your self-talk to sound kind and reassuring like you'd speak to a small child or a good friend. Why? Because more positive self-talk creates an inner supporter who generates energy, is an ally in creating what you want in your life, and builds you up when you falter. With this enhanced internal capacity, doing your good work in the world becomes easier: going for the promotion, taking a stand for your values, having the challenging conversation. And your inner landscape will become a refuge for replenishment rather than something to avoid and numb yourself against. Gone will be the energy, time, and emotional drain of continuously sword-fighting the negative.

When you become so accustomed to negative self-talk, it can be hard to find positive words. If that's the case for you, use the following examples as a jumping-off point. Notice that they model how to shift from negative self-talk to a positive version. The middle column indicates the unconscious need that may be driving the negative.

Negative Self-Talk	Unconscious Need[2]	Positive Self-Talk
Why am I always such an idiot?	Competence	"Whoops! I made a mistake here. I'm learning."
I can't do anything right.	Competence	"Every human messes up. It's okay."
I shouldn't go for this promotion. I may jeopardize my job.	Safety/security	"I've done lots of hard things, and it's safe to stretch myself. It's how I grow." "I'll be okay."
Everyone hates me.	Love/belonging	"I may not be for everyone. Not everyone is for me, either." "People close to me love me." "I'm not responsible for other people's feelings."
I'm fat, ugly, etc.	Love/belonging	"I'm beautiful inside and out. My flaws make me unique." "I love what my body does for me."

You'll notice that the positive self-talk isn't all sunshine and rainbows; it's just a more realistic appraisal of the situation that takes the larger context into account. This will help your system acclimate to the positive statements, rather than rejecting them as overly optimistic and wrong. If you still reject the positive thoughts as lies, remind yourself that we are *always* choosing our thoughts. And these thoughts create our feelings. You are choosing to believe the negative thoughts instead of the positive ones. And it's making you feel like crap.

Consider that your negative self-talk is usually expansive: "always," "never," "can't." There is a part of you that *knows* you are generalizing. No one is *always* an idiot. If someone paid you one hundred dollars for each example of you *not* being an idiot, you could come up with a list—and I bet a long one! Those positive examples are always there. Your brain is simply allowing in all the negatives and screening out all the positives.

If your system *still* rejects the positive options as lies, try "just the facts" phrases first, without the vitriol. Instead of the global statement, "Why am I always such an idiot?" try, "I wish that presentation had gone better" or "That email contained one spelling error." As your system adjusts, you can move to positive, reassuring self-talk.

Remember, you get to decide to start practicing different thoughts. Now. You are learning a new language, which means it will take time. That's okay. Your brain has been stuck in negative self-talk mode likely for decades. You are shaking up your neural pathways. And these new trajectories will serve you for the rest of your life.

4. INTEGRATE A PHYSICAL ACTION

When I am trying to integrate new positive self-talk, I often link it to a physical action that captures the emotional state I'm after. For example, as I was battling my inner doubts and fears about writing this book, I needed to feel capable, alert, and confident. I rolled my shoulders up to my ears and back down and said to myself, "You've got this." The action of rolling my shoulders back conveyed to my body that I was calm, strong, and ready.

When you repeat positive words often enough alongside a physical action, muscle memory reinforces the thought pattern for greater impact. Over time, you may find that merely the physical action suffices. I have noticed that there's a domino effect: The more we practice positive self-talk, the more other positive thoughts, feelings, and body sensations join the party.

The following chart walks you through the connection between the unconscious needs we seek, what we can say to ourselves, and how we can physically reinforce these sentiments. The ideas in the third column are merely suggestions; use the physical posture changes and actions that are most intuitive to you. Allow yourself a beginner's mindset as you try this brand-new way of thinking, speaking, and moving.

Unconscious Need	Positive Self-Talk	What to Try with Your Body[3]
Safety/security	"You are safe and well." "You have a roof over your head, food, and water. That's what matters." "This may feel scary, but you have what it takes to do . . ." "This situation may feel threatening because you're nervous, but you're okay."	Feel your feet on the floor and the solidity that's there. Notice your breath.
Safety/security	"Everything is okay." "Take a deep breath. You are calm and present." "All is well and as it should be."	Feel your feet on the floor, your back against the chair. Allow yourself to feel grounded and held. Bring attention to your breath. You don't need to change anything.

continued

Love/belonging	"Your body does incredible things." "You are loved the way you are." "You are an expression of inner beauty."	Place a hand on your chest and feel the vitality in your heart. Remember a moment you felt loved and imagine your heart warming.
Love/belonging	"You deserve to be here just the way you are." "Your being is enough." "You deserve to take up space and be the fullest expression of you in the world."	Cross your hands gently over your heart. Allow them to rest there and hold yourself.
Competence/ self-actualization/ meaning/feeling our place in the world	"You are great at . . ." "This is an opportunity to demon-strate your skill at . . ." "You've studied hard/prepared well/thought all of this through." "Remember all the times you've succeeded at . . ."	Bring attention to your spine and feel the strength that resides there. Straighten up and allow your chest to expand.
Competence/ self-actualization/ meaning/feeling our place in the world	"You can handle whatever comes." "Think of all the things you've suc-ceeded at." "You've got this." "You're prepared and ready."	Roll your shoulders down and back and open your chest. Straighten your spine. Place your hands on your hips.
Competence/ self-actualization/ meaning/feeling our place in the world	"Let's go!" "You're ready to make it happen." "Get psyched. Game time! You're on!"	Open your eyes wide. Inhale deeply and quickly exhale. Bounce a bit in your seat or on the balls of your feet.

EXERCISE > INTEGRATE POSITIVE SELF-TALK

1. Choose a few of the previous *positive phrases* that resonate
most—or come up with your own. Practice saying them out loud
to yourself three times each, along with a physical movement
that reinforces it. Notice the impact on your emotions, your body,
and your thoughts. Practice repeating the most resonate phrase
(along with the physical action) *three times* daily for one week to
internalize these beliefs.

2. *Think of a task* you've been avoiding or feeling fearful about. Create
a positive self-talk phrase that will settle your system enough to
generate peace and possibility from which you can take aligned
actions. Link a physical movement to the phrase to help it resonate
in your body. Practice the positive self-talk along with the physical
movement the next *five times* you work on the task. Repetition
will help the new pattern sink in.

3. Create structures that help you *remember to use positive self-talk
regularly.* Using Post-it notes, calendar reminders, alarms, and
screen savers are practical ways to remind yourself.

You have an incredible amount of power to create an internal experience of peace. It's simply a matter of choosing the practices that most resonate with you and using them until they become second nature. Consider how growing your internal peace will have a ripple effect on your family, your friends, your coworkers, and your community. If everyone used their capacity to self-generate peace, imagine how much less conflict and vitriol we'd have in the world. You're just the start.

Takeaways: Chapter Three

✓ **Self-talk** is the inner monologue of how you speak to yourself, and it has the power to radically transform your ability to feel internal peace. **Negative self-talk** is harsh, destructive, and unkind, and it depletes your energy. Conversely, **positive self-talk** builds you up, offers self-support to take on challenges, helps you identify and meet your own needs, dials down your nervous system, and provides a generative inner landscape to get replenished and restored.

✓ There are **four steps to improving negative self-talk:**

1. BE AWARE

Pay attention to the frequency of your self-talk, notice how often it's negative, and notice the physical effects of this negativity. Imagine these effects compounded over time.

2. NOTICE THE NEED

Your self-talk reveals an underlying need. Pay attention to what it is, and you'll have the power to use self-talk to meet your own needs.

3. INTENTIONALLY REFRAME

Change the tone of your self-talk from unrealistically negative to nonjudgmental and pragmatic, and—over time—to a loving and peaceful presence.

4. INTEGRATE A PHYSICAL ACTION

Associate an empowered action with your positive self-talk to move beyond words and fortify the mind-body synergy that generates a supportive inner landscape—a home base for your renegade spirit.

✓ You have an incredible amount of power to **create an internal experience of peace through positive self-talk.** This internal shift can expand your capacity and have ripple effects on your work, relationships, home, and community.

PART II

CATALYZE EXISTENTIAL PEACE

How many of us have become drunks and drug addicts, developed tumors and neuroses, succumbed to painkillers, gossip, and compulsive cell-phone use, simply because we don't do that thing that our hearts, our inner genius, is calling us to do?

—STEVEN PRESSFIELD, *THE WAR OF ART*

We've all experienced moments of existential longing. For me, it was being a mom of little kids and feeling strung out, hostile, and soul-weary from my career talents atrophying. Even when there were moments of joy, love, and play, I was still bleeding out. This is the kind of bone-deep dissatisfaction we experience when we shy away from the work of our dreams because of others' expectations, fear of failure, perfectionism, or internalized oppression. This form of suffering is like a gut punch of longing.

When this happens to you, it can be hard to put your finger on what the problem is exactly. Most people don't talk about existential dis-ease, so we have a limited frame of reference for this struggle. You might feel a nameless longing, or even a distinct sense that something is inherently wrong with *you*, when you are, in fact, yearning for something more and different from your life.

Existential peace is the result of living with purpose, honoring your values, and using your unique genius and talents to create what you long to see in the world. When we feel existential peace, our lives make sense on a soul level, and we feel well-used in the best sense of the word. And that feeling is grounded in fact. Research[1] suggests that people who have purpose in life live longer, enjoy better health, and are more resilient in the face of negative experiences. In the chapters that follow, we will walk through some of the most effective tools for identifying your purpose, values, and strengths in service of building a life filled with profound satisfaction.

Chapter Four

DANCE WITH MORTALITY

Mortality is a powerful catalyst to live purposefully. My husband needed a simple hernia repair surgery. He was going under anesthesia, an idea that evoked heart-seizing panic in me. My grandfather died during a heart procedure, and I was the one in the waiting room when the doctor called with the news. That experience looms over every hospital procedure for me.

In the days leading up to my husband's surgery, I ran various scenarios of how to manage his potential death. Where would we hold the funeral? How would the kids and I deal with it? What would I do with my regrets—the trips we hadn't taken, the times I'd been too tired for sex, the moments I hadn't savored? In the nights leading up to the surgery, I had nightmares of running out of money, not being able to fix a broken-down house, reaching for my husband's warm body in the night to find nothing. When he made it out of the surgery just fine, I committed to reinventing our relationship. I vowed to appreciate him more, relish our time together, be clear with my feelings, and have more sex.

This is the gift of mortality.

Dancing with mortality means regularly being aware of our mortality and recognizing its gift. If we lived forever, we wouldn't *do* much because there would always be a later—a later day, month, year, decade.

Mortality clarifies the sanctity and scarcity of the time we're allotted to live our potential, create the changes we long for in the world, and connect deeply with others.

> **Like those who've faced their own mortality, challenge yourself to use the time you have left to radically transform your worldview—and your life as a result.**

While mortality ensures that we honor life, many of us shield ourselves from the truth of mortality. We use chemicals to stave off aging, stay busy to the point of burnout, numb out on social and streaming media, and run from the big questions about why we are here. Lest you detect arrogance, I have been there too!

Can you include awareness of your mortality in your day-to-day life? Can you embrace it as an invitation to live full out, to connect with your legacy and purpose, to stand at the edge of your comfort zone and create what you're longing for? Yes, you can.

Inviting In Death

Western society tends to relegate mortality to hospitals, hospices, and nursing homes. But the COVID-19 pandemic brought mortality to our streets, our schools, and our homes. Day-to-day decisions became life or death. And in the years since the pandemic peaked, our collective awareness of mortality has fallen away again as we return to numbing ourselves into the worrisome delusion that death is a faraway prospect. But it's not.

To reconnect with the paradigm shifts available from centering mortality, how can you learn from the experiences of people who've already seen the beginning of their end? People close to death simplify their priorities. They become direct and clear in their communication. They center their genius, write that book, record that album, or take that public stand they've resisted. Even their relationship with time changes as they grow more aware of the inevitability of death. Paradoxically, as they become fully present and savor every small moment, deeply felt seconds can seem like hours. Moments with a loved one can feel timeless. In this suspended state, there are boundless opportunities for the things that matter most: connection, relationships, forgiveness, and self-compassion.

Like those who've faced their own mortality, challenge yourself to use the time you have left to radically transform your worldview—and your life as a result. Consider it this way: If you made a habit of recognizing your own mortality every day, what would change? I'm not talking about being stricken by panic or imagining your last breath—that would be paralyzing for most people. What I mean is allowing mortality to be a gentle dance partner with a hand on your back, nudging you out of the cushiness of your comfort zone into the edges of possibility because this is your *one* shot at life.

COVID-19 has given us all a near-death experience, if not the experience of actual loss of a loved one. Remember how the early days of the pandemic helped us reprioritize what mattered to us? We all felt the urge to spend our time differently, be thoughtful about our consumption, do work that matters, enjoy our relationships—all of it. Think back to that time in your own life. What was important to you when you weren't sure what would happen next? What were you most concerned about losing?

In much the same way, I am inviting you to dance with your own mortality now, before external pressure forces you to in the form of illness, tragedy, or uncertainty. Take this opportunity to make a deep and critical inventory of your deepest yearnings. Now. Write them down in your journal.

Learning to Dance

To truly dance with mortality means:

- Understanding the power of presence to magnify our experiences

- Being present to the life that pulses within us

- Asking what that life wants for us

- Recognizing the gift of health, developing an awareness of how stunning our bodies are, and appreciating what they do for us

- Refusing to give in to fear and other self-limiting habits that prevent our magnificence from being realized

- Fully expressing ourselves through living our purpose, avoiding the distractions of fear and needless worry

So many of us move unconsciously through the days, weeks, months, and years of our lives. We are ruled by our calendars, obligations, errands, social media, and others' needs. We may wish the days away until we get a better job, make it to the weekend, go on vacation, weigh ten pounds less, have grown children, get promoted, or hit retirement. But by then, our time is done.

Instead, let's use mortality to remind us to deepen relationships, do purposeful work, and create from the best in each of us. In this way, we can begin to quell our longing for existential peace—because we have embraced our temporary existence and what we truly want to experience from it.

EXERCISE > MAKE MORTALITY REAL

There are mortality apps that estimate how much time you have left. If that works for you, great. Personally, I find the experience of using them to be stressful. They activate a sense of panic and dread, which triggers an impulse to overachieve and isn't helpful for me. So, how can you regularly remind yourself of your own mortality (and that of those around you) in a gentle, life-giving way so that you harness your gifts in service of your purpose?

Experiment with the following ideas. Pay close attention to which of them inspire you without generating too much fear or anxiety.

- When you wake up in the morning, think about how grateful you are to be alive. Place your hand on your chest and feel the beating of your heart.

- Hold on to your vision for your legacy. What do you want to create in the world through your actions, relationships, and who you are as a human? You can create a vision board for this, journal about it, write the story of your life as you envision it, or even write your obituary. Then keep this content present by posting it visibly, rereading it, or having it pop up on your computer or phone at regular intervals. See page 84 for more about ways to identify your legacy.

- Calculate how many days you've been alive. How many of those have been well spent? If you're ready to increase that number, consider what actions or changes would bring more intentionality to your time. Be gentle with yourself. You are starting anew. No need to shame yourself for decisions of the past because they've helped you arrive at today. Put your new changes into

continued

action and check in with yourself a week later. How much of
your time have you spent being intentionally present?

• Journal about the following: If you were to die tomorrow, what
regrets would you have? Consider adventures not taken, words
not expressed, times when you let fear rule your life. If you
knew you had two years to live, what would you change? Let
this realization catalyze your actions.

Takeaways: Chapter Four

✓ Many of us move **unconsciously** through the days, weeks,
months, and years of our lives, taking for granted that **death** is a
faraway prospect.

✓ The COVID-19 pandemic provided humanity with a **near-
death experience** that forced many of us to confront our own
mortality and to reprioritize.

✓ Awareness of **mortality** is a gift. It invites us to connect with our
legacy and purpose and break free of our comfort zones.

Chapter Five

FIND YOUR SOUL'S WATER

You can create a powerful, purposeful life with greater intention. You can protect yourself from getting sucked into the unconscious blur of modern life. But work, practice, and deep attention are required. If you're willing to commit to the excavation and honest self-reflection required to discover what brings your soul deep and resounding peace—and in turn, what sucks you dry of purpose and joy—the potential rewards are boundless. Imagine how your days will feel infused with passion, fulfillment, and delight. Can you touch the ease of living in alignment with all your unique you-ness? I can't imagine a better way to spend a life.

The Four Steps to Existential Peace

1. CLARIFY YOUR LEGACY

Get clear on your *why*—your purpose, your reason for being, your soul's expression, your life's imprint.[1]

2. USE YOUR UNIQUE GIFT AND STRENGTHS

Determine what your unique capabilities are, and use them on purpose.

3. LIVE IN INTEGRITY WITH YOUR VALUES

Identify and align with your values so you experience the momentum of full integrity.

4. GET GOING

None of these insights do any good without action. Stave off inertia and make moves to be in sync with your legacy, gift, and values. Like, now!

Why Clarify Your Legacy?

Following the COVID-19 pandemic, many people decided that their jobs lacked purpose, appropriate pay, and healthy working conditions. These jobs weren't worth the burnout, commuting time, and emotional drain. People began craving work that aligned with their purpose and honored their talents and genius.

Many of my clients emerged from the pandemic knowing what they *didn't* want but struggled to identify what they *did*. Fortunately, this is where purposeful legacy comes into play. It's the friction of discontent and the sense of mortality that catalyzes us to discover our purpose.

We each have a legacy to offer the world that is the truest expression of our gift, experiences, and essence. I believe that if everyone fully expressed their potential, we could make a meaningful impact on challenges such as climate change, racism, hunger, and public health. People would work and live with more ease, pleasure, joy, and impact. Life wouldn't be utopic, but it would be substantially more fulfilling than how many of us live now.

This may sound like an oversimplification, but consider when you see someone "in flow." It might be a musician, a surgeon, a hairdresser, or someone giving a TED Talk. In flow state, a term coined by Mihaly Csikszentmihalyi, the individual effortlessly calls upon expertise they've honed, experiences timelessness, feels joyful, is fully immersed in the task at hand, and feels "in the zone."[2] As a witness, you can tell they possess synergy, excellence, and rapture. Imagine if each of us operated like that in the realms we care most about. The ripple impacts of our respective legacies would be astounding. I get goose bumps when I think about it. It's a future I'd feel proud to hand off to my children.

Legacy has different meanings for different people. For some, a legacy can be a relationship, a single action that makes the world better, or a way of being in the world that has a positive effect on people. For others, legacy is a giant weight they carry to measure every decision against. This was the case with me for a long time.

There's a concept in Judaism called *tikkun olam*, which roughly means "repairing the world." It has become intertwined with social justice, activism, right action, and social responsibility. In my culturally Jewish family, that concept translated to "make the world better." But in my brain it became, *You've had privilege, so you* must *serve.* That mindset instilled in me an unhelpful approach: feeling like I was running out of time to make a big impact, driving myself too hard in jobs focused on service, believing I was never doing enough, and experiencing restlessness because my purpose remained elusive. Enter rampant anxiety, burnout, insomnia, and full-blown breakdown.

What I want to offer instead is the whisper of legacy, by which I mean tuning in to what your true self, essence, or soul wants for you. When we connect with our legacy, our true purpose, there's often a deep resonance in our bodies, as if interlocking pieces have slid into place. Some people experience this connection in their solar plexus, like being pulled toward something. Others experience it as a lifting in their hearts or a longing in their abdomen or pelvis. You may experience it as a full-body sigh of relief and a settled feeling. Whatever the physical imprint, you know it when you feel it.

Hearing the Whisper of Legacy

You might feel just an inkling that you are meant for something more. Or you might feel the drumbeat of time driving you to engage in your life's purpose *right now*! Or perhaps you feel a sense of urgency alongside an expansive sense of time and the knowledge that you are part of humanity's long story. I call these feelings a *whisper of legacy*. I find this quote from Reverend Jen Bailey to be a great illustration of this concept:

> *"I can pass on that which came to me as seed, as blossom,*
> *and let somebody else plant it and tend to it. And that is so freeing.*
> *And if I could go back and talk to a younger version of myself,*
> *I would say, 'It's okay to not build the whole house.*
> *It's okay to lay a foundation and be satisfied in that.'"*[3]
>
> —REV. JEN BAILEY, GUEST ON THE *ON BEING* PODCAST WITH KRISTA TIPPETT

Although you can only do so much in your lifetime, you can use this limitation to fuel the momentum to pursue your legacy. Consider the feelings of stuckness and dissatisfaction as signals to inquire about your purpose and what you're longing for. Using a logic-based approach, answer these questions:

• What have you always loved to do?

• What brings you joy?

• What are you doing when everything feels "right," like your talents are used well and you feel a sense of deep fulfillment?

• What do you most wish to contribute to the world before you die?

• What do you want people to say about your life after you're gone?

• Which whispers of legacy have you been aware of?

If these questions are insufficient, you are likely bumping up against the limits of your rational mind. That's completely normal. What's called for instead is deep wisdom, intuition, and expansion of what's possible. That's where visualization comes in.

Visualizing Your Legacy

Visualization is one of the quickest tools to access your inner wisdom and intuition while preventing logic from getting in the way. Visualization employs an almost meditative state to activate your imagination, enable loose associations, and seed unique insights. Your senses soften, your breathing slows, and outside worries fall away as you focus more deeply.

I have seen visualizations unlock deep understanding, change people's relationships with themselves, and tap into the confidence of inner knowing. There's no right or wrong with visualizations. Trust that you'll get whatever you need, whether it's clear to you in the moment or not. For some people, immediate insights will come. For others, days later they'll have a new perspective or idea. Still other folks will experience serendipity afterward: a conversation with someone new that connects with their legacy, or an opportunity that presents itself.

This all may sound like woo-woo to you right now. However, we've all experienced becoming newly aware of something, and then we see it everywhere. We get a particular bike and suddenly notice all the other people riding the same one. We become pregnant and think, *Wow, there sure are a lot of pregnant folks in my town.* Or we fall out of love and suddenly we see only our ex's flaws. There's a biological basis for this. A brain circuit called the *reticular activating system*[4] is known as the "gatekeeper to consciousness." It regulates which external stimulation (visual, tactile, and the like) we pay attention to—or ignore—and how readily we react to different stimuli. Visualizations help prime your brain to notice experiences and opportunities that align with the legacy you identify. Once you recognize these prospects, you can start bringing your legacy to life.

EXERCISE ⟩ DISCOVER YOUR LEGACY[5]

Complete the following visualization and write down the answers to the questions contained within it as you go. Allow yourself to free-write—do not edit or read over what you have written until the end. Let the pen move, expressing the insights and answers that come effortlessly. It's often easier to enter a meditative state when *listening* to a visualization. You can find an audio version of the visualization on my website: www.therootedrenegade.com/resources.

If you struggle with visualizations, you may try instead to write a journal entry or record a voice memo, responding to the following questions. This practice will work even better if you quiet your mind before you begin. Try not to think too much about what you're writing. Just jot down whatever pops into your mind.

1. Complete this visualization. Feel your feet on the floor and take three deep breaths in and out. If possible, exhale for longer than you inhale. Imagine that you are sitting in a room bathed in golden light with an older, wiser version of yourself. This version of you has been there, done that, and has come to share their insight with you from a place of deep love, care, and wanting the best for you. In this moment you are comfortable, relaxed, and eager to hear what they have to say. Ask your older, wiser self the following questions:

continued

- What am I meant to do?

- What does life want from me?

- During my lifetime, what will I feel most proud of having contributed to my community, my loved ones, and my work?

- What do I most want to offer the world before I die?

When you've finished with these questions, ask your older, wiser self, "What is the best way to access you in the future?" Listen for the answer, then thank them for sharing these insights with you. Feel your feet on the floor and your back against the chair. Take a deep breath in and out and come back to the present moment.

2. Read over your responses. Then ask yourself, "What is my legacy?" Write the answer in your journal. Iterate until the description of your legacy resonates deeply within you.

3. Read your legacy out loud three times. Notice your emotional response and the physical sensations in your body as you do so. These are the imprints of your legacy's longing to be expressed in the world.

4. Journal about any changes you want to make to your life to align with and further your legacy.

If you're looking for more resources about discovering your legacy and purpose, consider delving into the Japanese concept of *ikigai*, or your reason for being. It is the intersection of what you're good at, what you love, what the world needs, and what you can be paid for.[6]

Genius Is Waiting for You

I sat in the back row at a friend's violin concert. Even at that distance, I was transfixed. Her bow barely touched the strings. Her fingers coaxed the sound with micro-adjustments to the violin's neck. Her torso met the undulations of the music.

We all have the same genius within us. Yes, you too! The range of human talents is breathtaking. From artists and healers to cleaners and manufacturing whizzes. There are types of genius people possess that we don't have jobs or industries for . . . yet.[7] For any need we humans or the planet has, there are other humans for whom doing that thing is as easy as breathing. Unfortunately, many of us aren't tapped into our gift, much less living the expression of it in the world. The cost is restlessness, untapped potential, loneliness, and thoughts like *Is this all there is to life?*

Michael Meade is a storyteller and mythologist who works with at-risk youth to call forth their genius. He believes that children's genius is evident even in preadolescence; he sees philosophers, masters of words, and many other gifted young people among the kids he serves.[8] Meade notes that children try to express their genius, but it can be shut down by their families. I see this in myself and my clients when we trace the roots of our genius back to what we loved to do as children—and felt successful at—before someone told us it was frivolous or we couldn't do that for a living.

In my own children, their genius is readily apparent. But it's their choice whether they ultimately embrace and nurture it. My older child was born with a deep empathy for others. They know when someone is in pain, even when that person masks their distress, and they intuitively have insight about people's internal emotional landscapes. This gift could result in them becoming a therapist, coach, sociologist, or philosopher. My younger child is skilled at communicating with and training animals, even stubborn ones, and is naturally musical and artistic. She could use these talents to become a vet, singer, fine artist, music teacher, or pet therapy trainer. Whether my children take one of these paths is up to them, but their innate skills mean that these paths would be more easeful.

Often a high-achieving client comes to coaching with an insatiable inner stirring, a feeling that something is wrong or missing. They've tried to adjust their schedule, practice more self-care, or seek out different jobs, but nothing scratches the itch. When we excavate together to identify their longing, we often discover that their genius isn't being used. Even if they are doing work that aligns with their legacy (medicine, education, academia, law—all noble pursuits), their day-to-day tasks crush their spirit. Their essence is yearning to live out its purpose *and* express genius. Its language is existential angst. Author Gay Hendricks deems this the "Call to Genius."[9]

My guess is that you are highly successful at work. You perform the tasks demanded by your job and you achieve at high levels within your industry. You likely are well regarded by your peers, and the work itself doesn't feel unduly difficult (though it may feel hard to integrate life and work and balance all of your job responsibilities). Hendricks refers to this as the "Zone of Excellence." You can go through a life like this but miss out on the ease, fulfillment, and joy of what Hendricks deems your "Zone of Genius." This is the work that gets you up in the morning, has you racing to your desk, feels easy, and launches you reliably into the flow state.[10] In flow, time passes quickly, tasks feel effortless, and you're "in the zone." The Zone of Genius aligns with your legacy. Part of the work of a lifetime is discovering your genius and believing you are entitled to live in a way that centers your genius.

So what's getting in the way? We are unskilled and unpracticed at asking ourselves and others what we are good at. We live in fear. We worry about what our families, friends, and colleagues would think if we were audacious enough to fully step into our gift. And we're too busy on life's hamster wheel to take the time and energy to align with our gift. We may minimize our genius because it seems too "easy" or not "special." Sometimes, we don't believe we are entitled to feel joy, pleasure, or fulfillment. Internalized capitalistic values only further influence us to acquire things over our own existential peace. Success and pride can block us from pursuing our genius, because why change anything if our lives are "working" from the outside? Only when internal existential angst (or boredom, stuckness, or restlessness) becomes all-consuming or we have a mortality scare do many of us realize that we need a fundamental change.

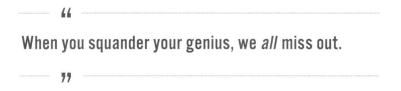

When you squander your genius, we *all* miss out.

Confronting the reality that you haven't been living out your legacy and genius can cause grief and regret. You also may fear compromising your success and disappointing others. You may wonder: *What if I can't make money doing this? Am I selfish pursuing this when other people can't? What if I am not good at this? Do I deserve ease and joy? What if I let people down?*

And yet, I've found that time and time again, once a person identifies their genius and recognizes their legacy, it's hard to turn away from them. They've tasted their soul's water and nothing else will sate them. Their genius becomes a branch point in their life from which crucial moves are born and fulfillment takes root.

When you squander your genius, we *all* miss out. What could be more powerful and gracious for yourself, others, and the planet than fully stepping into what you're meant to do? So do all of us a favor and take the time to discover your genius by completing the following exercise.

EXERCISE > UNMASK GENIUS[11]

As you complete this exercise, there may be a temptation to focus solely on work. That's okay, but I also invite you to view your life expansively: relationships, family, hobbies, and so on. To come into a fuller understanding of your genius, journal about the following:

1. What did you love to do as a child? Think back and get specific here. What about that interest did you love? Consider the activities, how you felt, who you were with, and what stands out the most.

2. How does that same activity or skill show up in your life now?

3. What type of work or activity puts you into a flow state where you lose yourself and feel soul-level satisfaction? Be specific.

4. Which skill, strength, or capacity elicits intense jealousy from others? (This might be clear from body language, words, or actions.)[12] Alternatively, which of your capabilities inspires others' admiration?

5. Reflect on your answers from 1–4. What particular skill or trait stands out? Consider this as the key to your genius. To flesh this out, get as specific as you can. Your genius is not just "helping people" but instead "excavating people's deepest, unspoken desires." Not just "teaching" but instead "translating complicated concepts into

continued

playful ideas so kids can access them." Being specific makes it easier to see when you're using your genius, to claim that genius as yours, and to make aligned choices.

It may help to go through these questions multiple times, each time getting more specific and nuanced. You may consider having a friend ask you these questions or recording a voice memo for yourself. Hearing your answers aloud may evoke a different reaction.

Read through all your responses, in particular what you said about the things you loved doing as a child. Then, answer the following questions:

6. What is your gift or genius?

7. When you think about the legacy you identified, how does your gift serve your legacy?

8. What actions will you take to focus on your legacy and use your genius more?

Living Your Strengths

Whereas your genius is a singular skill, gift, or talent that is tied to your purpose and legacy, you have many strengths spanning different life domains. Every day becomes *so much easier* when you honor and build upon your strengths (instead of investing lots of time and energy battling your weaknesses). Consider how a performance review at work feels when squarely focused on improving your weaknesses versus expanding your strengths. This is a countercultural notion in a society that prizes perfection and optimization over personal fulfillment.

As a result, sadly, many of us never recognize our strengths and gifts. Because they are easy for us, we invalidate their importance.

Case in point: I was helping to hang bunting decorations for my youngest child's graduation ceremony. Now, I possess neither the crafty part of the human brain nor the part that understands dimensions, estimates distances, and visualizes how something will look. I'm not kidding—I scored 5 percent in spatial awareness on an aptitude test in high school. As I struggled, another parent issued commands and constructive criticism:

"Down a bit more . . ."

"These two lines won't fit . . ."

"Let's attach the wall hook here . . ."

"Those won't align . . ."

"You're really good at this," I told her.

"I don't know about that," she answered.

"You've never been bad at it, so you don't realize how good at it you are!" I replied.

"Hmm, I never thought about it that way," she said, chuckling.

And that's how many of our strengths are. They elude us when we don't take the time to name and claim them.

EXERCISE ❯ NAME AND CLAIM STRENGTHS

Take a moment to list your strengths. When I ask people to do this, they often write down five to ten items. I want you to aim for at least thirty. Bring it!

Here are a few questions to help you start sourcing, noticing, and listing your strengths. Journal your answers so you can refer to them later.

continued

- When you feel joyful, what are you doing? Which strengths are you using?

- When you're in flow, what are you doing specifically?

- What are you doing when you feel most yourself?

- Which of your strengths are obvious?

- What do people say you're good at? (Consider what your partner, family, boss, colleagues, and children say—yes, even the little ones, you'll be amazed at their responses.)

- Ask your friends, "What am I really good at?"

- Which qualities do you bring out in others?

- What did you enjoy and rock at as a kid? (Look at this one expansively. If you used to make painted rocks and wheeled them around the neighborhood selling them, you might have strengths in creativity and entrepreneurship; if you argued skillfully to stay out late as a teen, perhaps you have strengths in advocacy, public speaking, or writing; or if you loved building crazy towers out of blocks, you may have strengths in design, vision-setting, engineering, problem-solving, and spatial skills. Examine your earliest experiences and what you came back to again and again in your free time.)

Keep in mind that you can get stuck when attempting to acknowledge your strengths, if your inner critic becomes activated. It may say things like, "No, you don't really have that strength" or "Who are you to think you're good at that?" or "But remember the time you sucked at that?"

continued

If you hear such voices as you attempt this exercise, then first take a moment to list your inner critic's common phrases (it will help this part of you feel heard and, hopefully, chill out). We all have an inner critic. Left unchecked, it can be a pesky bugger. It is trying to protect you and help, but its methods are terrible. Try to send your inner critic some love and ask it for some space to do this exercise. For more about the inner critic, see To Change Something about Yourself, Love It First on page 151.

If you're still feeling stuck, there are other ways to access your strengths. Consider taking the VIA Survey of Character Strengths,[13] which helps rate your relative strengths with a research-backed survey instrument. It's quick and easy. You can also look over previous performance reviews. Only note the positives! What is consistently called out as a strength you possess? Finally, you can commit for one week to write down where you have excelled and what has come naturally for you. If you're the data-driven type, track which strengths you employ, and how often, over the course of a week.

Reorient toward Your Strengths

One of my clients did the previous exercise and realized that most of her work tasks were not in her areas of strength. She spent lots of work time struggling with things she found challenging, such as budgeting, processing invoices, or managing projects. No wonder she was feeling unsuccessful! This mismatch led to frustration, inefficiency, and her team not getting the best from her. She was inspired to talk with her boss about reallocating job responsibilities across the leadership team. She also recommitted to clear boundaries around when to say no to tasks with diminishing returns. As she reoriented her job description, others on the team aligned their responsibilities with their strengths. The experience normalized and made transparent that everyone on the team had strengths and challenges.

> **"**
>
> ## Train your brain to see your strengths more often than it sees your weaknesses.
>
> **"**

When you start honoring your strengths more, you spend more time in sync and less time banging your head against the wall. (Please don't ever actually bang your head against the wall—it is one of your most precious resources!) Of course, you *can* work on your weaknesses, but if you spend most of your time doing that versus building upon your strengths, you will work much harder than you need to. Work and life can feel *easy*, and it's not cheating.

One outcome of noticing and reorienting toward your strengths is to train your brain to see your strengths more often than it sees your weaknesses. This counteracts the human negativity bias, or tendency to focus on the negative, and rewires your brain to see your wholeness, capacity, and resourcefulness.

Look back at your list of strengths from the previous exercise and let yourself take in how magnificent you are. Soak them in! You walk around with these strengths wherever you go. You have the capacity to impact the world and others using these skills, whenever you want. Pretty incredible, right?

EXERCISE > CENTER ON STRENGTHS

Now look at your list of strengths and estimate how much of your time you spend using them. With that information in hand, journal your answers to the following questions:

1. How would your life change if you used your strengths intentionally and daily? What impact would you have? How would your relationships shift? How would your quality of being change?

2. How will you focus on paying more attention to your strengths? Some examples:

   • Tell a friend, partner, or colleague what you're up to and ask them to share when they see you using a strength.

   • At the beginning and end of each day, spend a few moments thinking about your strengths and what they will offer you or did offer you that day.

   • Look at your strengths list once per day.

   • Get creative: Use posters, notes, or mantras.

Align with Your Values

Your values form the fabric undergirding your life because they are the non-negotiables of your heart and soul. When you act in alignment with your values, you tend to feel grounded, calm, and in sync. You may recognize this in the satisfaction you feel donating money or time because it honors your value of service. Or it's the groundedness that comes when you return an overpayment because it aligns with your value of integrity. Failing to honor your values causes friction, undermines your peace and integrity, and leaves everything feeling "wrong." But honoring your values, on the other hand, brings coherence to your life.

Values also impact how you make sense of your experiences, big and small. For example, imagine a driver weaving in and out of traffic, making you feel enraged. What's frustrating you isn't simply that the driver is being dangerous. Instead, spurring your upset might be values such as order, adherence to rules, respect, consideration, cooperation, or community. Another person encountering the exact same behavior might think, *Wow, they're efficiently moving through traffic* or *Nice move* or even *That's Boston for ya.* That person likely values innovation, efficiency, or autonomy.

Values always remind me of a quote from the movie *Dirty Dancing*: "Nobody puts Baby in a corner." Values hidden away or dishonored will make themselves seen! When clients bring up the challenges keeping them awake at night, there's often a conflict of values at play. You probably see this in your own life, too, when your friends, colleagues, and loved ones struggle. It's the lawyer working in biotech but worried whether patients can afford the drugs (made more expensive by the firm's fees). It's the CEO planning layoffs and imagining how families will suffer. It's the teacher unable to meet all the needs of students in their classroom.

One of my favorite questions to help illuminate values is: "What drives you nuts or keeps you awake at night?" Underneath the frustration, irritation, or sleeplessness are values that are being dishonored. If your partner leaving socks on the floor makes you nuts, you might have values of consideration, order, cooperation, neatness, and beauty. If poor grammar makes you want to tear your hair out, you might have values of achievement, consistency, competency, and predictability. When politicians' budgetary decisions cut funding for veterans, you might feel irate if you hold values of fairness, justice, service, and respect. You get the idea—when something bothers you, look for the values at play.

Many of us only tune in to the emotional experiences of events, actions, and contexts and stop there. We don't look behind what's *driving* our responses. When you are unaware of the values that motivate you and help you make sense of the world, you miss opportunities for alignment and set yourself up for frustration and angst. This kills peace.

EXERCISE 〉 IDENTIFY YOUR VALUES[14]

It might feel elementary or obvious to explicitly identify your values. However, I've seen that when clients are clear about their values, they can more easily identify priorities, make aligned choices, and understand complex circumstances.

1. Identify your *five* most important values. Refer to the following list as a starting point.

   Achievement, adventure, advocacy, ambition, authenticity, autonomy, beauty, belonging, caring, collaboration, community, compassion, contribution, control, cooperation, courage, creativity, curiosity, diversity, ease, education, empathy, equity, excellence, family, flexibility, forgiveness, fun, honesty, humor, inclusivity, integrity, kindness, leadership, learning, loyalty, nature, openness, optimism, order, perseverance, playfulness, pleasure, productivity, religiosity, seeking, spirituality, success, transparency, travel, zest.

continued

If you have difficulty identifying your values, consider the following: How do you spend your time, what do you spend money on, what makes you nuts, what keeps you awake at night, whom do you admire (and why), what values do you think all children should learn, and what needs in the world are you moved to meet?

2. What does it look like when you honor each of these five values? What does it look like when you dishonor each one, and at what cost?

3. How can you lean even more into your values on a regular basis? Consider work, relationships, home, hobbies, your spiritual life, and the small moments in your day.

Get the Hell Out of Your Comfort Zone

Our comfort zone is a delicious place—like a tub of ice cream or a perfectly cushy couch. But you don't find existential peace devouring tubs of ice cream or scrolling on your couch. Your brain likes to tell you often that you are safe in your comfort zone. There is no fear of predators, social humiliation, failure, or suffering. And yet, if mortality were standing over you, it would say, "Get the hell off the couch!"

> **"**
>
> ### It's the chafing against comfort that yields impact and exponential advances.
>
> **"**

No legacy is realized, no internal gift is fully expressed, and no meaningful change in the world happens from your comfort zone. If that were how it worked, then we'd always express our gifts and legacies. Rather, it's the chafing against comfort that yields impact and exponential advances. When you experience the discomfort of pursuing your legacy, remind yourself that's how it's supposed to feel. Be with those feelings, allowing them to move through you. Then settle your nervous system by generating internal peace, remind yourself of the legacy you're after, and claim who you're committed to being in the world. Take one tiny step forward. Then rinse and repeat.

Takeaways: Chapter Five

✓ There are **four steps to creating existential peace** on your terms:

1. Clarify your **legacy**.

2. Use your unique **gift** and **strengths**.

3. Live in integrity with your **values**.

4. Get **going**!

✓ You have a **legacy** to offer the world that's the truest expression of your **gift, experiences, and essence**.

✓ **Legacy** has different meanings for different people. For some, a legacy can be a relationship, a single action that makes the world better, or a way of being in the world that has a positive effect on people.

✓ You can identify your legacy using logic, but **visualization**—a tool that bypasses your thinking brain—can be more effective.

✓ Everyone has **genius**: a talent or skill so innate and effortless it often exists just below our conscious awareness. Identifying and tapping into this gift is essential for achieving fulfillment and existential peace.

✓ In addition to a singular genius, each of us has many **strengths**. While society often tells us to focus on improving our weaknesses, building on your strengths is a more stable and reliable path to happiness, success, and existential peace.

✓ Taking an inventory of your strengths and **realigning** your work and life to emphasize them will counteract negativity bias, train your brain to engage more with your strengths than your weaknesses, and seed greater resourcefulness.

✓ **Values** are the non-negotiables of your heart and soul, so values-alignment will help lead you toward existential peace. If you have difficulty identifying your values, study situations that make you upset and reflect on what values you feel are being dishonored in those situations.

✓ While your **comfort zone** provides a feeling of safety, it does not nurture growth. To advance your legacy, you must leave your comfort zone!

Chapter Six

MOTIVATE WITHOUT FEAR

Many internal forces can motivate you toward a conscious life that has you leaning out over the edge of your skis, living fully in service of your legacy, expressing your genius masterfully, and not tumbling down the mountain into the abyss. But how? It starts with honoring both your small and large successes and making peace with fear through self-compassion. Then you advance to adopting powerful perspectives and mindsets, seeing your resourcefulness, and making moves that your nervous system is ready for.

Honor Small and Large Successes

I was talking with a client who worked in a leadership position within a large organization. Despite being a successful and powerful woman, she often felt frustrated and depleted, which hindered her ability to engage in the organization-level change work that she aspired to pursue. I asked how she regularly acknowledged and celebrated her wins and successes. "I don't need a party when I do my job," she insisted. "This is what I'm supposed to do."

Although reluctant at first, she was willing to experiment with paying attention to her wins. We made it into a game, which felt lighter and kept her resistance at bay. Over time, she recognized that she felt better when owning her successes. *Win!* More than that, she became more motivated to try out new approaches and take risks. Because she created a well of confidence to draw from, it became easier for her to make the bold moves she was longing for, even when they felt uncertain or scary.

Many of my clients who are at the top of their fields share this common pattern: They hold on to all their failures, setbacks, and negative feedback while discarding their wins, contributions, and positive feedback. At best, their daily balance of emotional reserves is zero. For many, it's a negative balance. Either they do everything perfectly today and manage to creep a bit past zero, or because they are human, they make errors and thus their negative balance drops even more. The next day, it begins again. *Oof!* This is an exhausting pattern to endure. I know because I lived for a long time with that dragon breathing down my neck. The energy it takes merely to remain at baseline crushes any possible momentum toward your legacy.

If this sounds like you, don't beat yourself up. Humans tend to gravitate toward the negative, which has helped us survive over thousands of years. If we forget what hurts us, we might die from it the next time. And if everyone did that—*poof!* Humans would be gone. You can acknowledge that you're wired this way and still work to change these default patterns purposefully.

Much like the gratitude practice earlier, sitting with your wins does not look like jotting down a list and moving on. Instead, it means taking stock of what you've done; allowing yourself to experience the sensations of accomplishment, pride, and contribution; and recognizing that *you* did that! Some people find that keeping a list of wins, filling a jar with their wins written on slips of paper, or planning celebrations to honor their wins can serve as potent reminders of their accomplishments. These practices can build up confidence and motivation to draw upon when taking challenging action toward your legacy.

And you don't have to wait to accumulate wins! Allow yourself to celebrate your wins in the moment they happen. BJ Fogg, author of *Tiny Habits*, invented the term "shine" for the emotion you experience when you have a win. He has loads of ideas for in-the-moment celebrations that evoke "shine": doing fist pumps, humming songs, having private dance parties, and the like. Allow yourself to experiment, get silly, and identify what feels celebratory to *you*.[1]

Like the client I mentioned previously, you may worry that focusing on your wins will lead you to "rest on your laurels," "get lazy," or "be unable to achieve." You've internalized these messages from our capitalistic society, parents, colleagues, or even your internal mechanisms. Notice the similarities of the worries here with those we covered in Chapter Three, Four Steps to Improve Negative Self-Talk on page 62. While this kind of hard driving may have pushed you to achieve at high levels—just like rampant negative self-talk—it can come at a cost: an inner world that feels like torture, self-imposed stress, and physical ailments.

"What got you here won't get you there," as Marshall Goldsmith, the renowned author, business educator, and executive coach, says. "There," in this scenario, is your legacy—but without constant self-recrimination and suffering. Instead, you'll get there by celebrating your accomplishments, supporting yourself with positive self-talk, honoring your values, and leaning fully into your genius and strengths.

EXERCISE > CLAIM YOUR WINS

As a start, journal your answers to the following questions:

1. What is a win you had this week? The size of the win doesn't matter. Take a few moments and write about what happened, including as much detail as you can. You did that! What impact did you have? Allow this win to soak into your body and be aware of the physical sensations.[2] You might notice your chest warming or expanding, your muscles relaxing, or your posture settling. Whatever it is, just notice.

If your inner critic gets activated and starts to yell something like, "That win didn't count"; "Yeah, but you didn't do this part well"; "But what about . . . ," remember that is normal. Your inner critic is used to minimizing your wins. It is experiencing uncertainty and fear about trying something outside your comfort zone.

This is an opportunity to do something different. Take a deep breath in and out and feel your feet on the floor. Try one of the breathwork exercises from Part I. With your nervous system calmer, invite your inner critic to give you a moment to experience what this win feels like. For more about the inner critic, see page 151.

If your system is particularly resistant to acknowledging your wins, try sitting with tasks you've completed each day that, at a minimum, didn't suck. You can inch your way toward recognizing the value of your wins with this practice over time. Remember that your resistance to enjoying your accomplishments isn't "the truth." It's just a thought. *You* get to decide which thoughts you pay attention to and which you allow to wash over you as noise.

If you need more support identifying your wins at first, recruit

continued

an ally such as a friend, a partner, or a colleague who can help you see where you're killing it. As you become more practiced at seeing your wins with the help of a buddy, you'll learn to do it for yourself.

2. If you were to make a regular practice (daily, weekly) of celebrating your wins, how would you function differently at work? How would your quality of life change? What would become possible?

Take the Steam Out of Self-Generated Fear

We have an incredible capacity to scare ourselves. It's as if our imagination goes off the rails and turns against us. Consider how often you imagine negative outcomes rather than positive ones.

One helpful strategy for managing your fear comes from Jack Canfield's *The Success Principles*. He encourages people to use this framing: "I want to____, and I scare myself by imagining____."[3] More simply, you can just say, "I'm scaring myself by imagining____." The brilliance here is in acknowledging that you are *making up* all the reasons to be fearful.

You likely have the experience of getting stuck in a thought-loop, rehashing the same fearful or negative thoughts like a skipping record. In fact, research shows that we have thousands of thoughts each day and the vast majority are repeats![4] I am exceptionally skilled at thought-loops: *Will my seventeen-year-old get into the college they want? Will they be happy there? What if they don't have friends? Will they know how to study for tests? Will they take the classes they need for their major? What if their advisor is terrible? Will they pass their classes? What if they drop out?*

Your brain thinks it's keeping you safe by chewing on the possibilities, anticipating contingencies, and gaming out options. That might be the case if you contemplate these matters a couple of times (and act based on insights). However, these thoughts cycle through your brain hundreds of times. Thought-loops do way more harm than good. They are distracting, distressing, and disempowering.

> **"**
>
> **When you connect deeply with the present moment, you realize everything that matters most is fine.**
>
> **"**

When I realize I'm thought-looping and don't like how it's making me feel, I employ a wacky strategy, but it helps. I imagine the thought traveling through neurons in my brain on a well-worn path. Then I picture a stop sign and sometimes physically put my hand up to indicate "stop." I say, "Stop. I don't like how this feels." Then I imagine a new pathway for a new thought. I call up a reassuring, calming thought instead—something I'm grateful for, a dose of self-compassion, or a neutral spin on the situation I'm looping on. My brain will want to return to the thought-loop because it's a well-grooved route. The practice is to continue to shift and redirect so that a new, more life-giving thought takes root instead. Over time, this new thought will become the easier path.

Finally, when you connect deeply with the present moment, you realize everything that matters most is fine. Your breath happens, your mind thinks, your colon digests, and you aren't in imminent danger of harm. You can return to this present moment again and again when fear tries to take hold.

EXERCISE > REWIRE THOUGHT-LOOPING

Identify something you're thought-looping about. Then ground yourself. Feel your feet on the floor, your back against the chair. Place your hands on your legs and notice the solidity there.

Read the following:

Stop! I don't like how this feels. This thought-looping is a habit my brain likes to do. It doesn't mean any of these worries are true. I'm scaring myself by paying attention to them. Thinking through this endlessly will not lead to a solution. Instead, I'm going to think, *All is well at this moment* or *I am capable and strong* or *It's okay, honey; you're just scared.* If none of these resonate, pick a different reassuring thought.

Choose an activity that occupies your body and/or mind like listening to music, calling a friend, cooking a delicious meal, reading a book, or going for a run.

Recognize When Failure Has You

When you're afraid of failure, guess what you're actually afraid of? *Yourself.*

How's that? When you make a mistake or fail at something, the tangible consequence (e.g., criticism, a late submission, a disappointed colleague, an error in a document, a challenging conversation with a boss) lasts only for a moment. What last much longer are shame, self-loathing, self-beratement, and rehashing. This can go on for a long time. You have the capacity to change this pattern by recognizing that you cause your own suffering and therefore can drive your own peace.

Learning from failure requires you to examine where you've fallen short. If your nervous system is keyed up, your likely response is to avoid looking at your failures. I've seen clients do this with hobbies, presentations, challenging conversations, and performance reviews. This results in so many missed learning opportunities. In fact, studies show that we learn optimally when we make errors 15 percent of the time.[5] I don't know about you, but I never celebrated an 85 percent on a test (except in physics!). But if we eschew our errors, we miss the opportunity to forge new connections in our brain and develop greater skill and efficiency.[6]

When you're able to settle your nervous system through self-compassion, calming breaths, and positive self-talk, you can create space from your negative thoughts and view your failures as opportunities for growth. So, if the only thing waiting for you on the other side of failure is learning and self-support and care, what is there really to lose?

EXERCISE ❯ CHECK YOURSELF

Journal about a time that you failed at something.

- How long did the *actual* consequence last (e.g., the difficult conversation, the report card you received, the difficult feedback)?

- How long did you berate yourself (e.g., a moment, night after night, years off and on)?

- The next time you fail at something, how do you want to speak to yourself? And how will you support yourself instead of causing your suffering?

The Power of a Perspective Shift

Having read this far, you've probably noticed that I experience life through a personal development lens. This means my nightstand is filled with self-help, leadership, and psychology books. When I read the news or watch television or movies, I look for nuggets to share with my clients or incorporate into speaking engagements. My kids tell me, "Get a life!" My response is always, "May you love *your* job this much one day!"

Seeing the *small* shifts in mindset or perspective that make *huge* impacts for my clients is one reason my job lights me all the way up. So, I'm accustomed to looking for perspective shifts, which is why an episode of *Chef's Table* on Netflix stood out to me. It featured Dario Cecchini, a butcher and chef in Italy, who approached his work with gusto, joy, and passion.[7] Watching him in his convivial restaurant made me want to insert myself into the TV.

As explored in the episode, Dario originally wanted to be a veterinarian. He was deeply connected to animals, and when he looked into their eyes, he felt called to take care of them. But while Dario was attending veterinary school, his dad, a butcher with his own shop, got sick and could no longer work due to his illness. Dario was pulled between pursuing his longing to become a veterinarian and his duty to his family. He ultimately left school.

Dario wrestled with how he could possibly butcher animals after he had felt so connected while caring for them. He felt downtrodden, frustrated, and stuck. He feared disappointing his family but was stymied by how to make peace with his gruesome new line of work. The person who was responsible for animal quality control for the family's business told Dario (paraphrased): "You are taking care of these animals as a butcher by ending their life cycle in a way that honors the life they've lived and their ultimate sacrifice. You're treating this animal with the respect it deserves."

When you select an empowering perspective, it unlocks the motivation to fire up your life with less fear.

This shift in perspective led Dario to see his life and mission completely differently. It unlocked his inertia. He became instrumental in the culinary nose-to-tail movement, honoring all parts of the animal. He began to love his work and imbued joy into his shop and the restaurant he would eventually open. Dario's radical perspective shift stemmed from a few sentences that changed the trajectory of his life and caused ripple impacts in the food system in Italy and throughout the world.

Like Dario, we all get locked into perspectives—often without realizing it. Usually what you think are immutable facts are simply perspectives. Your perspective or thoughts lead to your emotions, which create your actions. When you select an empowering perspective, it unlocks the motivation to fire up your life with less fear.

If existential peace is a priority for you, then focus on cultivating perspectives that serve this end. Imagine how many perspectives you are holding that, if shifted, could break through your inertia and catalyze your legacy and genius. A simple perspective shift could change your life and the lives of those around you!

EXERCISE > SHAKE UP YOUR PERSPECTIVE

Journal your answers to the following questions:

1. Where are you stuck in a perspective that limits access to your legacy and genius? Look especially at where you are feeling disempowered, victimized, or negative.

2. Which other perspectives are available to you? Brainstorm alternatives. Consider those that are radical, out-of-the-box, positive, and nuanced.

3. Identify which perspective you want to adopt by looking at the emotions and actions each creates.[8]

Surprise! You've Already Figured It Out

When your nervous system or thoughts inevitably resist the challenges that come with living your purpose, you can settle down by connecting with your inner resourcefulness. To that end, I'm about to say something radical, so brace yourself: You've already solved every challenge you're facing right now. Before you throw this book across the room, stick with me here. This is a new way of thinking about your challenges, one that is anchored in your own capability. Regardless of how you may feel or what your thoughts tell you, no circumstance at its root is novel to you.

When a client faces a supposedly new challenge, one of my first questions is often, "How have you figured this out before?" The answer may lie in a different part of life that they hadn't connected to the current challenge. Often, it's a question of decontextualizing or generalizing the challenge so they can witness their resourcefulness in a new light. There's seldom one right way to solve a challenge. The most effective way is your own unique way that reflects your individual gift and talents and aligns with your values.

Let's use an example many parents experienced in the past few years: navigating remote learning for your children during the pandemic. Now, had you ever experienced a pandemic before and had to manage the day-to-day schooling of your child, while still working your job? No. But notice how context-dependent and specific the setup appears. Compare that to the familiarity of these generalized versions of the same challenge:

- Had you ever worked from home (including during or after work hours) prior to the pandemic?
- Have you ever worked to support your kids with learning at home (homework, projects, reading, etc.)?
- Have you ever had to balance working and parenting demands?
- Have you ever had to shift your schedule because of a life change (e.g., having a baby)?
- Have you ever dealt with an uncooperative child?
- Have you ever navigated stressful situations?

Of course all these situations feel much more familiar. Stripped of their hyperspecific context, the elements of the "novel" problem are clear. The roots of your solution have already been planted in how you've navigated analogous situations. Breaking down a new obstacle into its most general and familiar elements rewires your brain from self-doubt to resourcefulness.

EXERCISE > SEED RESOURCEFULNESS

When you hear yourself saying, "I don't know how to do this" or "There's no way I'll solve this," make a habit of using the following questions. Then you can start reminding yourself, "I've figured this out before."

Think of a challenge you're facing that feels novel. Journal your answers to the following questions:

1. What are all the similarities between this "novel" situation and others you've handled?

2. How have you figured out something similar before?

3. What skills did you use in those prior situations?

4. How did you execute?

5. What worked and what didn't?

Success Starts with a Tiptoe

An incredibly creative client was struggling to fully move toward her dream of entrepreneurship. She'd get inspired, make a move, but then panic because it felt like too big a leap. This led to a rubber-band effect: She would lose motivation, self-doubt would enter, and she'd struggle to build herself back up again. To help her break out of this pattern, we used the frame Tiptoe, Big Step, Leap to make more sustainable progress. It is a mindset, an invitation, and a recognition that small moves and small successes create the foundation for the bigger reaches beyond your comfort zone.

What looks like a tiptoe to one person might be a leap for someone else, so know thyself. Identify what fits for you at each level: What's a tiptoe toward your legacy? What's a big step? What's a leap? Then start small and allow each tiptoe to lead you to the next big step, and each big step to reveal the path forward to a leap. And don't forget to celebrate the hell out of yourself for each tiny bit of progress along the way to boost motivation *and* infuse joy into the journey.[9] Be conscious of the gentle hand of your mortality on your back, urging you to continue walking up to the precipice of a bigger life for yourself.

I incorporated this practice myself when starting my coaching business. At first, it felt like a big leap, and reflexively, self-doubt crept in. But instead of giving up, I focused on tiptoes toward my goal bit by bit. I began by filling out the LLC paperwork to formally become a business. It was a piece of paper and a check, nothing more, but it was a signal to myself of my legitimacy in the eyes of the state. I'm risk averse, so the next bigger step was getting business insurance. Then I thought: *Well, now that I have my LLC (and I'm protected by insurance), I have an official name and can get clients.* I was ready for the big leap of creating a website. Each tiptoed step gave me the boost of confidence needed for bigger action. The big step then felt like the next natural move, not a giant risk. With each bit of progress, I inched toward my legacy of supporting people—toward living a conscious, fulfilling life. As you grow in your confidence, you may find that what was once a leap becomes a tiptoe.

Consider that as you take each step, the universe rewards you. It's the job opportunity that arises just as you've polished your resume. Or the banker who gives you a special deal when you open your first business account. Or the email to become a foster parent after you decided to make a difference for kids in need. Similarly, as you begin to take your tiptoes, the footholds to the legacy of your dreams will start to appear.

You'll notice the following exercise integrates the lessons of previous chapters, including physical postures and movements, positive self-talk, your legacy, and starting small to build momentum.

EXERCISE ❯ SET YOURSELF UP FOR SUCCESS

Journal your answers to the following questions:

1. When you think about your legacy, what are the tiptoes, what are the big steps, and what are the leaps? Identify three tiptoes to take in the next week. Then allow yourself to bask in these wins after you've achieved them.

2. What's an affirmation that will remind you of your legacy and your capacity to generate the existential peace you crave? Create a physical posture or stance that locks in this sentiment. This will support you to take your first tiptoes, big steps, and leaps.

   Examples of affirmations:

   • "I am taking this tiny step to move closer to my legacy of . . ."

   • "This little step will be simple. Imagine the huge impact of my legacy of . . ."

   • "I've already done . . . ; now I'm simply taking on this next step."

Getting Out of Your Own Way

Even with your best plan in place and the smallest tiptoes, you can still covertly get in your own way. We can't leave this topic without talking about the many-headed beast of self-sabotage: procrastination, overcomplication, perfectionism, complacency, and squandered opportunities. Oftentimes we self-sabotage because we fear getting what we want. This might sound counterintuitive, but it's true.

When I first started my coaching practice, I wanted a waiting list of amazing clients, a six-figure income, a team of coaches working for me, and retreats and speaking gigs all over the world. But when I imagined achieving that, panic consumed me: *Will I ever see my kids? Will I get burned out? Will I still love coaching? How much time will I spend managing versus my true love, coaching?* Not until I imagined arriving at my goal did these deep fears become clear. Previously, my subconscious fears had undercut efforts toward my goal. But once I named these worries explicitly, they loosened a bit.

In the presence of fear, we self-sabotage. We also self-sabotage in the absence of self-trust. To manage my fears, I needed to develop my self-trust and recruit different types of support. First, I had to own my capabilities and build my confidence. As detailed in the previous chapter, I excavated my genius and strengths. I paid exquisite attention to (and celebrated) my wins. Over time, these incremental steps led to greater self-trust. I made the choices *I* wanted in my business instead of prioritizing others' wants and needs. And I understood that I wasn't in it alone. I cultivated relationships with allies, colleagues, teachers, and mentors whom I could call on for support.

Self-sabotage can masquerade as "intuition," "a well-thought-out decision," or even "truth." This dynamic is ripe for coaching, as it is entangled with self-confidence, feelings of efficacy, perspective, self-talk, and other issues of personal growth (many of which we've covered in previous sections).[10]

EXERCISE 〉 TAME SELF-SABOTAGE

1. Identify your self-sabotaging patterns. Do you procrastinate/ avoid? Overcomplicate? Change directions quickly or abandon your plans? Let opportunities pass you by? Or each of these in different contexts? Keep a list of these handy.

2. When you see something, say something. If you notice any of these self-sabotaging patterns, tell on yourself *lovingly*. "Sweetie, you're self-sabotaging." "Oh, look at that. It's my self-sabotaging again."

3. Identify your fears explicitly. Notice if there are basic needs (e.g., safety, belonging, or competence) beneath the fear. If so, go back to the exercise in Chapter Three, Four Steps to Improve Negative Self-Talk on page 62. Otherwise, confront the fear head-on. Ask yourself, "What am I afraid of?" Get specific and clear. If that doesn't work, ask yourself, "What do I want most?" (e.g., a raise, promotion, new job, success in a side gig). Then imagine you've gotten it. You're there. What comes up? Notice any negative thoughts or emotions.

   If any explicit, logistical, actionable concerns come up, address them. In the previous example with my concern about burning out, I made a commitment: I will take on no more than twelve clients at a time. I listened to the fear and addressed it. If you're afraid of failure, plan for what happens if you fail (and how you'll build yourself back up).

4. Manage the fear by trying the following exercises:

   a. Relax your body using the exercises in Chapter One.

continued

b. Once you're relaxed, honor your fear as a self-protector. Reassure it that you've addressed the fears head-on. Listen carefully to see if there are any other fears that haven't been named and addressed.

c. Remember your strengths and wins! List them to connect with the badass in you.

d. Get support from your allies, colleagues, friends, family. Be explicit about what you need.

e. Practice exceptional self-care—whatever helps your body and soul feel calm, relaxed, and refreshed.

5. Connect back to your legacy and get to it! Remind yourself of your legacy and how this action relates to it. Then take your tiptoes.

6. What did you discover about how your self-sabotaging operates? This self-knowledge will grow over time to support you in shifting your self-sabotaging patterns. And if new patterns emerge, work through the previous steps.

Takeaways: Chapter Six

✓ **Celebrate your wins!** This will not make you lazy. Instead, it will provide you with a well of emotional reserves that will make growth outside of your comfort zone feel easier.

✓ Innate negativity bias often leads to **imagining negative outcomes** rather than positive ones. By maintaining awareness of negative thought-loops and mindfully engaging with your body, you can disrupt these negative cycles and allow your mind to find new, more constructive pathways.

✓ When you're **afraid of failure**, you're actually afraid of yourself. By calming your nervous system, you can create space from your negative thoughts and view your failures as opportunities for growth.

✓ Your **perspective** informs your emotions, which inspires your actions. Selecting an empowering perspective will unlock inertia.

✓ You've already **figured out every challenge** you're facing. Regardless of how you may feel or what your thoughts tell you, no circumstance at its root is novel to you. Breaking down a new challenge into its most generalizable parts will help you recognize problems you've already tackled—and solved—in the past.

✓ **Tiptoe, Big Step, Leap** is a useful framework to push the edges of your comfort zone. Start small and allow each tiptoe to lead you to a big step, and each big step to reveal a leap you're ready to take. Remember to celebrate along the way. Don't bite off more than you can chew, but do be conscious of the gentle hand of your mortality on your back.

✓ **Self-sabotage** can take many forms (e.g., procrastination, overcomplication, perfectionism, complacency, squandered opportunities), but it often stems from the same root: fear of getting what you want and a lack of self-trust. To overcome this fear, you must understand your fears, develop your self-trust, and recruit support.

PART III

UNLOCK RELATIONAL PEACE

It's the quality of our relationships that determine the quality of our lives.

—ESTHER PEREL

Relational peace consists of three key areas: your relationship with yourself, your relationships with others, and your relationship with the world. Your relationship with yourself is foundational and vital. If you experience distress, beratement, and rupture in this relationship, it's nearly impossible to feel peace whether you are on the beaches of Bali or in the depths of meditation.

Your relationships with others fill out the contours of your life. If your relationships with others run amok, it's difficult to feel settled and spacious. To achieve relational peace, you can examine which relationships serve you—and which don't. You can articulate boundaries that support you and can manage relationship breakdowns authentically.

Your relationship with the world impacts your spirituality and the security you feel walking through life. It defines your perceived place in the span of humanity, how much authorship you feel over your life, and whether you feel like things work out and the universe has your back.

Chapter Seven

DISCOVER YOUR RELATIONSHIP WITH YOURSELF

If you haven't caught on to this message so far, let me reiterate: You're amazing. I know it because every human I've ever encountered is, and you're no exception. What will it take for you to internalize that about yourself? Understanding your life's journey so far and how it has contributed to creating the unique being you are today can help. We get so caught up in the day-to-day that we seldom carve out the time and space to gain perspective on our life from a 25,000-foot view. That stops now. This understanding is a springboard for self-appreciation, self-respect, self-love, and self-honoring choices and actions.

You're going to work up to creating a life map, a visual representation of your life's journey. Your life map includes the good, the bad, the ugly, and the beautiful—all of you. If you took away any one of these parts, you wouldn't be who you are today.

When you're in the middle of any life experience—challenging or elating—it feels all-encompassing. In these moments, it's hard to step back and appreciate how it fits in the broad swath of your life experience. This is why it's helpful to create a life map to integrate all of it and take time to let insights about yourself unfold. This can catalyze the beginning of a richer, more nuanced relationship with yourself.

When I run workshops to help people create life maps, participants often realize how much they've grown and changed. They've been surprised to realize how relatively short their tougher moments were. They unpack broader themes like gaining confidence, claiming their identity, or reckoning with a challenging upbringing. My hope is that some of these deeper insights unfold as you create your life map.

What I have seen in my clients and myself is a tendency to either dwell on or outright reject our darker moments. This causes us to get stuck emotionally or in negative thought patterns about our more challenging moments. We have a huge opportunity to step back, see the lessons, and excavate the gold within them. Then we understand how these moments sit alongside our high points, learnings, and themes of our journey. Allow yourself the space to welcome these moments onto your life map.

EXERCISE > CREATE YOUR LIFE MAP

1. IDENTIFY ESSENTIAL EXPERIENCES

List *at least* five essential life experiences you've had.

Consider the following prompts to help identify your essential life experiences:

- Experiences that brought you immense joy

- Accomplishments you're most proud of

- An experience that if you took it away, you wouldn't be you

- A massive failure or disappointment[*]

- Highlights from your life that would appear in your obituary

- Something you are embarrassed by or wish had never happened

continued

2. USE CREATIVITY TO DIVE DEEPER

For *each* of the five experiences you've outlined, do *one* of the following:

- Write about it (poem, journal entry, song).
- Create a drawing, painting, or collage that presents the experience.
- Record yourself talking about it.
- Use any other creative pursuit you'd like.

3. REFLECT

Look back over your creative exploration and journal about the following:

- Did any of your perspectives shift or deepen?
- If your perspectives didn't shift or deepen, what's a new perspective you'd like to hold about the experience? Remember, perspective is a choice, even if it doesn't always feel that way.
- What insights did you gain?
- What did creativity offer you?
- Are there other places in your life where creativity could serve you?

4. GAIN PERSPECTIVE

This step coalesces everything from the previous steps to create a life map—a visual representation of the story of your life, including both high points and low ones. You will be able to look at it again and again to glean insights and perspective. The components of your life map can include your five essential experiences; any major events (e.g., job changes, moves, schooling); demographic changes (e.g., births, marriages, deaths); shifts in your personality or priorities or major personal

continued

insights; moments that stand out in your memory; and anything else that feels important. Your map may have zigzags, squiggles, branches, dips, and rises—anything goes. You can organize it chronologically, by theme, or in any other way that makes sense to your brain. Sometimes people struggle with this activity because there aren't concrete rules or guidelines. If you're having trouble getting started, just start with your birth and proceed chronologically. There's no right or wrong here. It may serve you to make several iterations of your life map because different visual representations can spur unique insights. For visual examples to inspire you, go to www.therootedrenegade.com/resources.

To give an example, looking at some of the major events, experiences, and insights of my own journey, my life map would highlight the following:

Being an extremely sensitive little kid, combating anxiety and depression in my teens and twenties, my parents divorcing in my teens, attending the college of my dreams, being in a serious college relationship that was soul-redeeming and ultimately broke my heart, studying psychology, moving to California on my own after college, meeting my husband, going to law school, getting diagnosed with a chronic illness, having my first child, and so on.

5. IDENTIFY YOUR THEMES

Once finished, look across your life map and take it all in.

a. Narrate aloud the story of your life, walking through the life map. You can do this by yourself, record a voice memo, or share it with someone you love.

b. In a quiet moment, journal about the following related to your life map:

• Which themes do you notice?

continued

- What stands out to you or surprises you?

- What gifts has your journey given you?

- What are you able to offer the world *because* of the journey you've had?

---

* Note: Please don't deeply explore and wade into trauma without professional support. Doing so could cause you to become retraumatized.

Uncover Your True Essence

The life map you created in the previous exercise represents the broad swath of your life. Here we will deep dive into the essence of *you*. The story of the Golden Buddha of Thailand (*Phra Phuttha Maha Suwanna Patimakon*) is instructive here. Hundreds of years ago, a golden statue of the Buddha was built for a temple in Thailand. When unrest and theft threatened the statue in the eighteenth century, it was covered in stucco and colored glass to protect it from being looted by foreign invaders. Over the generations, people forgot that it was ever golden. Some two hundred years later, the statue was being moved during construction when a piece of plaster fell off, revealing the gold beneath.

In this same way, we are all golden at our core; this is our essence. Life cruds over our gold. Experiences and messaging entrench unhelpful mindsets and narratives. Trauma dims us. Messages from parents, school, friends, and society tell us to stay small and safe. Structural racism, homophobia, transphobia, sexism, fat phobia, and other bigotries tell us we are only valuable if we exist in a particular way. Many forces work to dull and diminish our magnificence.

When I first start working with a client, I see a glimmer of their gold. Together, we clear the crud so that more of their gold can shine again—for themself and for the world. They discover what they are truly capable of and how powerful they are. It's like witnessing a mystical unfolding.

Just like with my clients, I'm *not* okay with you walking around crudded over.

We have all experienced moments when we can touch our essence. It's the quality of being that you exude wherever you are. It's the magic of you in all your you-ness. It's the quintessential part of yourself that often gets lost in the day-to-day. Some examples of qualities of essence are: brilliance, courageousness, effervescence, empathy, ferocity, idealism, imagination, inquisitiveness, intuitiveness, joy, mischievousness, openness, playfulness, resourcefulness, spaciousness, spunk, tenderness, truth-telling, vivaciousness, warmth, wisdom.

Your essence is the place from which your authentic wisdom and insight speaks. It's the voice that says, "This is what you're meant to do"; "You know"; "You are loved." It is *not* the voice of ego that wants success, material items, or power. It's also not the source of tirades, the inner critic, the Monday-morning quarterback, or the part of you that worries about what others will think. Instead, your essence shows up in those serene moments when you are deeply in touch with yourself. It guides you and loves you. It simultaneously honors where you are and knows your power.

Where in your body does your essence emanate from? Take a quiet moment and notice where you feel it. It might be your heart, head, solar plexus (just below where your rib cage meets), belly, abdomen, pelvis, sacrum, or any other part of you.

EXERCISE > GREET YOUR WISE ESSENCE[1]

Go to my website, www.therootedrenegade.com/resources, for an audio version of this exercise.

Place your feet firmly on the ground and take three slow breaths. Breathe in all the way to your belly and then exhale, letting go. Again, inhale all the way to your belly, and exhale, letting go. One more time in, then out.

Imagine that you are traveling to a place in nature where you feel calm, peaceful, powerful, and fully yourself. It might be the desert, the ocean, a forest, a meadow, or a mountaintop—anywhere you fully connect with yourself and the world around you. Imagine that you are in this place now. Take in the smells, the sounds, the light falling on the landscape. Notice the calm in your body.

There is a trail next to you. You walk down it with a feeling of antici-pation. A figure comes toward you. You are about to greet your essence. Notice how they are dressed and the energy they exude. They are excited to meet you. As your essence approaches you, notice what it's like to be in their presence. How does your body feel? Take an inventory of your head, neck, shoulders, heart, belly, abdomen, legs, and feet.

Your essence is about to answer some questions. As it speaks, notice the place in your body from which the voice emanates, or where it resonates. Place your hands there as you ask the following questions and listen to the answer from your essence:

- Who am I at my essence?

- What do I need to know?

- What will my life look like five years from now?

continued

- What direction should I go in?

- How can I connect with you easily and often?

- What else? (You have endless creativity here to ask anything you wish. Just listen.)

When you've heard what you need to hear, know that you can connect with your essence anytime you wish. Thank your essence for being there for you now and for your whole life going forward. Feel your feet on the floor, your back against the chair, and come on back.

Then, journal your responses to the following questions:

- Which positive characteristics did your essence have? Make a list.

- Which other characteristics would you add that seem completely you?

- Which messages from your essence stood out to you?

Evoking Your Essence

Just as in the previous exercise, we each have special places that call forth our essence more easefully. It might be basking in the noises of the city or standing at your kitchen sink. Most commonly, these settings are in nature:

- The seaside—beach, ocean, marshland, bay

- The mountains—vistas of mountains, seeing above the tree line, fresh air

- Bodies of water—lakes, rivers, streams, babbling brooks, expanses of waterways

- The desert—barren views, starkness of life, hills of sand, dry air

- Forests—the scents of pines, the rough-hewn paths, the filtered light

Most of us don't access our essence sitting in traffic or biding time at the DMV. You get the picture.

For greater insight about your true essence, you can ask yourself, "Who am I at the _____ (beach, forest, desert, city center, etc.)?" Note the aspects of your personality, strengths, energy, and orientation toward life that show up effortlessly in these spaces when you are most yourself.

Locking in how you feel in the locations with the most direct access to your essence is crucial. That way, if you are scared, operating from ego or your inner critic, disconnected from yourself, or prioritizing others' needs over your own longings, you can imagine your special place and create the body postures and sensations of being in the place where your essence reigns.

The beach is the place where I feel most myself and most tapped into the larger world around me. At the beach, my essence comes out in my actions, quality of being, and energetic experience. These are the qualities of essence that emerge when I am at the beach:

CURIOSITY

I look for sea creatures, new shells, and different types of seaweed, and I ponder the ways of nature.

INNOVATION

Whether it's wrapping a stranded puffer fish in seaweed to launch it back into the sea, angling beach umbrellas against the wind, or outsmarting crafty seagulls, I am creative here.

INSIGHT

My best ideas come to me at the beach: business ideas, a theme for an article, a program I want to put together. Ideas pop up constantly while I walk and allow my mind to wander. The bigger questions—those existential ones that usually sit just behind our consciousness—come to the forefront for me to rest in and mull over. My mind exists on another plane there.

AUTHENTICITY

I am most *me* at the beach. I have cried there, laughed there, connected with my husband and friends, and yelled into the wind.

The beach is my essence's anchor. I can lock in the physical sensations of this place and how my essence is when I'm there. You will discover more about your own essence in this exercise.

EXERCISE 〉 GROUND YOUR ESSENCE IN PLACE

Identify the place where you feel most yourself, most alive, most grounded, or most present. Imagine this place or even look at a picture of it.

- How are you holding your body as you picture this place?
- What are the sensations you experience here?
- Which positive traits and characteristics are present when you're in this place?
- When you're here, what do you dream of?
- What thoughts occur to you here?
- What's available to you from your essence that supports your legacy?

Connect with Your Essence on the Regular

As you regularly connect with your essence, you can access your inner voice and inner wisdom more intentionally. Quieting down and listening are crucial. In the chaos, frenzy, and endless chatter of life, it's hard to hear that quiet, steady voice. Yet it is your inner compass. How can you know what you truly want and where you are going if you don't take time to listen to the wisdom of your essence?

When my clients make this listening a regular practice, they drop seamlessly into their inner knowing when they want or need it. It is beyond your regular intellect and more in the realm of intuition, calling, soul, or spirit. Trust that as you connect with this inner knowing more and more, your access to your own wisdom will deepen. This is your deepest relationship with self.

Make a commitment to connect with your essence, to listen to it, and to visit the places where you feel most connected to it. Take a stand that you won't go another day without mining the wisdom of your essence and walking with it more consciously through your life. Greater peace awaits when you change your orientation to focus first on your essence. The rest will fall more naturally into place.

EXERCISE › CONNECT WITH ESSENCE

Connect with your essence every day this week. As previously outlined, you can do this by sitting quietly and imagining the place where you regularly feel your essence; holding your body in a way that evokes the qualities of your essence; touching the place on your body from which your essence seems to emanate; or reading the list of essence characteristics you developed. Ask your essence, "What do I need to know?" Even if it's hard to connect inside, sit in quiet anyway. You may have an insight later on that stems from this moment of quiet and connection with yourself.

Meet Your Inner Pit Crew

A part of our incredible inner resources and support is what I call our inner pit crew.[2] This is the cast of positive personality facets contained within us. Imagine what a pit crew does in a long-distance race like the Indy 500. Each member of the crew has a specialty: changing the tires, doing a tune-up, strategizing with the driver, refueling, and so on. Each person is uniquely trained, competent, and focused on the task at hand. The driver can count on each member of the pit crew to support them to complete the race successfully and safely.

Similarly, you have a constellation of personality facets that help you get through your day-to-day, week-to-week, year-to-year. An essential aspect of relational peace is getting to know these parts of yourself, becoming familiar with their specializations, and learning how to call on them. In doing so, you cultivate allies for life.

This concept can feel abstract, so here are some examples of inner pit crew members you might have. The possibilities are limitless! As you review this list, see which of these are familiar aspects of your personality. Claim these pit crew members as your own.

- Optimist
- Idea generator
- Creator
- Problem-solver
- Cheerleader, supporter, parent
- Spiritual advisor
- Number cruncher
- Logical one
- Environmentalist
- Nourisher
- Guardian of the body
- Doer, action-taker
- Motivator
- Comedian
- Learner
- Romantic

You will notice that all the previous examples are *positive*. We do have parts of our personality that are responsible for protecting us against all manner of imagined ill fates. They often do so in unskillful ways such as negative self-talk, doomsday scenarios, avoidance, and the like.[3] But for now, focus only on the personality facets that *support* you.

One of my pit crew members is a cheerleader. Which makes sense, because I was a cheerleader in middle school—a fact that shocks people who know me now. This part of me shows up when I motivate others when they are feeling frustrated, stuck, or uninspired. When I call upon this part of me purposefully, I am positive, energetic, and even effervescent. You might see me singing or dancing. The trick is to understand this part of me, remember that I have it, know how to activate it, and apply it when I need it.

Another one of my pit crew members is my spiritual advisor. It's the wise, calm, spiritual, intuitive part of me that knows just what to do. I've personified it as an elephant I call Ellis, which makes it more concrete and easier to access. When I seek spiritual insight, I look at an image of an elephant or I picture an elephant walking steadily alongside me. Instantly, my energy shifts, and I'm able to access insights and inspiration. As you discover and use your own pit crew members, you will notice how much more capacity you have to navigate different aspects of your life.

EXERCISE 〉 NAME YOUR PIT CREW[4]

Use the following prompts to generate names for your pit crew members, similar to the list of examples.

- When you read the list of possible pit crew members, which jump out as aspects of you?

continued

- When you're inspired, which inner parts of you show up?

- Consider what you are like at work, at home, or while you are engaging in hobbies or creative pursuits. Which pit crew members can you identify in these contexts?

- When do you feel like a badass? Which pit crew members are present?

- At your quirkiest, most playful and joyful, which pit crew members show up?

The Power of Accessing Your Inner Pit Crew

Often, you'll find that an inner pit crew member is confined to a particular domain of life by default. You can draw upon them in different contexts to get their full value as you wish. For example, I have a creative part of myself. It most readily shows up when I'm cooking. Let's call this inner pit crew member my chef. With my chef in charge, I am creative, I get into a groove, I can multitask, I'm energetic, and I use whatever's available in the fridge and make the best of it. Anything feels possible, and I'm confident the outcome will be delicious.

I feel the complete opposite when I am packing for a trip. I loathe packing. I wait until the last minute, trudge through it, panic, know that I won't pack the right stuff, and hate all my clothes.

If I allowed my chef inner pit crew member to pack, the experience would look radically different. I would see packing as a creative challenge. I'd mix and match, having fun with combinations. I would feel confident in my selections, and I'd bounce around my room with a sense of play and discovery. I might even *love* packing.

So how do I access my inner chef? If I picture myself cooking, I notice a few things: I'm light on my feet, almost bouncing. I have my headphones on, listening to a podcast, music, or news. I open the fridge with a flourish. My arms move effortlessly like an orchestra conductor.

All of the following clues are access points for this pit crew member:

- How I set up the environment: I listen to something that's interesting and gets my juices going.

- How I hold my body (posture): I lean forward slightly; my body is light and bouncy, not rigid.

- How I move my body: I'm like a conductor, with flowing, fluid movements.

Each of these access points can support me to get cheffy with my packing. I can listen to a podcast, lean forward, be light on my feet, and move my body in a flowy manner as I'm taking out my clothes. Embodiment is key here. And now packing will be easier and more fun.

However, going through TSA at the airport, I might opt out of employing my inner chef because it would be too casual and loose. But if I'm feeling bogged down as I'm creating the outline for this book, my chef could help. Or if I seek reflection and wisdom, I might call up Ellis by sitting back in my seat, slowing my breath, and allowing for whatever comes up. Notice how strategic I can be employing these parts of myself.

The more you understand your different inner pit crew members, the more choice you will have to deploy them. Your resourcefulness and confidence will grow. And your awareness of the full range of who you are will result in a robust relational peace.

EXERCISE > GO DEEP WITH YOUR PIT CREW[5]

Identify three inner pit crew members. For *each one*, ask yourself:

1. What is this pit crew member like and when do they usually show up?

2. What's my environment like when they are present?

3. How do I hold my body and move it when I'm connected to this part of myself?

4. Which thoughts and emotions does this pit crew member hold?

5. What are the contexts in which this part of me is helpful now? How might I invite this pit crew member to support me in different contexts?

Identify and Claim What You Need

Many of my clients, especially those who identify as women or other marginalized identities, were socialized out of recognizing, articulating, and prioritizing their needs (me too!). Perhaps you were told as a child that your needs didn't matter, or maybe you got the message to stay quiet and out of sight. You may have learned that self-sufficiency was equivalent to love. And society loves reinforcing that it is selfish or ungrateful or unfeminine to claim what you need and want.

What's the effect of this socialization (i.e., brainwashing)? You put your head down, get shit done, and subserviate your own needs to those of others. Over time, this practice results in losing trust and connection with yourself. A child who asks again and again to have their needs met only to be ignored ends up pulling away from the relationship. That's what happens inside each time you ignore your needs. You have the capacity to change this dynamic completely. Centering your own needs, recognizing them, and voicing them fortifies your relationship with yourself.

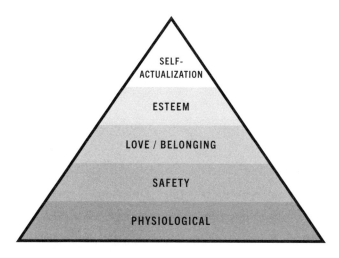

Maslow's Hierarchy of Needs

Maslow's hierarchy of needs[6] is a helpful place to start, as it's foundational to what all humans need, in order of priority:

1. Physiological: food, water, warmth, rest

2. Safety: security, lack of threat

3. Belonging and love: friendship, intimacy, connection

4. Esteem: achievement, accomplishment, contribution

5. Self-actualization: using our full potential, creativity, genius, gifts

It is difficult to move up to the next level until you've satisfied the more foundational level below it. For example, if you don't have food, you seldom prioritize love and belonging. Remember the earliest stages of the pandemic when it was unclear how often you could get to the grocery store, toilet paper was in short supply, and you didn't know how to protect yourself when you went out? During that time, you were less likely to focus on the next promotion at work (esteem) or whether your intimate partnership was satisfying your needs (belonging and love). Your system is wired for these ordered preferences.

When you face a challenge at a particular level, for many of us it becomes all-consuming. If you have a terrible fight with a partner—which triggers needs of belonging and love—you might get tunnel vision about it. You feel that it must be urgently resolved before you can focus on work or anything else. Similarly, if you're awaiting an important medical test result, you will be hyperfocused on health and safety, and that creative project you were excited about gets put on hold. Even if you are a person who compartmentalizes aspects of your life, you are likely feeling stressed, worried, and distracted outside of your conscious awareness when your more basic needs are threatened.

Stress can upend this hierarchy. When we become deeply stressed at work, for instance, we often skip meals and sleep, and we disconnect from others. The opposite is how we *should* be managing stress: getting good sleep, resting, and relying on our people for love and connection. Then we are well sourced to tackle higher-level wants and needs.

If truly thriving is represented by the top two layers of Maslow's hierarchy of needs, then you need to ensure that your foundational layers are covered. See how this works?

Transition from Surviving to Thriving

Once you've gained comfort knowing and articulating your needs, you can begin to uplevel from merely surviving to thriving. You know intimately what surviving looks like: working long hours or indulging in food, drink, drugs, shopping, social media, and television to numb out from the compromises that survival necessitates. For many of us, it's how we've run our lives for too long.

> **"**
>
> # The more you prioritize thriving, the more self-trust will bloom.
>
> **"**

Thriving is a different matter entirely. Your body and mind need to last your whole life. This is obvious, but when you get that deep in your cells, you understand that your frame of reference is the long game rather than day-to-day optimization. The more you prioritize thriving, the more self-trust will bloom—the felt sense and deepest knowing that you have your own back. In this context, you listen deeply to yourself, prioritize yourself, and recognize that you are unwilling to compromise your needs in the service of others' comfort.

Surviving Questions	Thriving Questions
What can I throw together for dinner the quickest?	What healthy food is my body craving?
How can I lose this weight?	What parts of my body need greater strength and flexibility?
How many cups of coffee do I need to stay up late to finish this article?	How can I plan ahead so that I'm not compromising sleep to get my work done?
Can I secure that promotion by working more hours and showing my commitment to the organization?	Can I secure that promotion by taking exceptional care of myself so that I'm mentally and physically clear?
How can I push through so I don't have to say no to my boss?	How can I honor my boundaries and communicate to my boss that this ask is too much?

EXERCISE › REFLECT ON THRIVING

Journal about the following:

- How does my body-mind-heart feel when I'm thriving?

- If I were the steward of my body-mind-heart for the long haul, what would be the non-negotiables?

Awaken Your Dreaming Capability

This is an invitation to rewire all that conditioning and recognize that you are worthy and entitled to *ask* for your dreams. You! You are the visionary, architect, and engineer of your life. To create an authentic life on your own terms, it's important to understand your fundamental needs (the baseline), then what you want (the nice-to-haves, the desires), and finally the ultimate dream (what brings your life to the next level where it feels like your soul is singing). Without an understanding of these three levels, you can easily default back to focusing solely on your needs and lose sight of the full range of possibility for your extraordinary life.

1. MINIMUM VIABLE NEED

This is what's required for you to function and go about your day-to-day life. It's the essentials and the non-negotiables.

2. WANT

This is the nice-to-haves, inklings of desire. These are the mid-layers of Maslow's hierarchy of needs (belonging, esteem).

3. THE OPTIMAL DREAM

This is your highest dream for yourself. You'd be joyful, fulfilled, ecstatic if this were realized. It's the highest level of Maslow's hierarchy of needs (self-actualization).

You can look comprehensively at the needs, wants, and optimal dreams in different domains of your life to clarify what you seek. Without knowing this destination, the powerful changes needed to get there will elude you.

EXERCISE ❯ KNOW YOUR NEEDS, WANTS, AND DREAMS

NEEDS

Think about something that you need to function—to go to work, take care of your kids, manage your day-to-day. It might be water, food, sunshine, sex, human interaction, money to pay your bills. Consider how it feels in your body to need this thing.

Let's take water as an example: What's it like to feel thirsty? You may notice a parched feeling like something fundamental is missing, a single-minded focus on attaining it, resolve and compulsion, even a grounded sense of deserving. There may be a strong desire to act or a heat in your belly.

- Based on this experience, what are the sensations of need within you?

WANTS

Now consider something that would be nice to have—something you desire or want. Life would be easier, sweeter with it. It might be a flexible schedule at work, a bit more time to play with your kids, or a nice trip

continued

with loved ones. Let's take a more flexible schedule as an example: What's it like to want flexibility, choice, autonomy? Pay attention to the physicality of this wanting. Your chest and belly may lift; you may lean forward, being arched on the balls of your feet; your brain might start to puzzle on ways to get it.

- Based on this experience, what are the sensations of wanting within you?

DREAMS

Finally, consider something you dream about that would bring joy, fulfillment, a next-leveling to your life, or a sense of wonder, "How is this possibly my life?" It might be a second home, a family of your dreams, bucket-list-worthy travel on the regular, an optimal partner who lights you up in all the ways, a business that is legacy-creating and earth-quaking. Let's use a second home as an example. Imagine your home: It's everything you've ever hoped for. The location is exactly where you want, the furnishings are perfectly selected, the feeling when you step inside is pure bliss. Bring your awareness to what it's like to dream about this wish. Your heart may lift and open, you may connect with elation or bliss, your body may feel relaxed or buzzy, or you may feel outside of yourself.

- Based on this experience, what are the sensations of dreaming in you?

Our brains can do something incredible: acclimate to new realities, and fast. This is how people are so adaptable and able to manage storms, pandemics, new normals, and pivots. As your needs are met, over time a higher bar (or baseline) becomes the minimum viable need. For example, let's say your need in relationships starts with not being yelled at by your partner. Over time, as you aren't yelled at, what may have started as a want—being treated with respect—is now a non-negotiable. Perhaps your new want then becomes having a partner who openly expresses love and commitment. This ratcheting up can occur in all domains, which will uplevel your overall quality of life. You will start believing that you are entitled to more, better, and different, rather than the bare minimum scraps you tolerated before. Woo-hoo to rewiring socialization!

When you initially make an upward adjustment, you may experience a shock to the system as you try to integrate it. Internal scripts crop up, which often sound like: "Who am I to want this?" or "Whoa, I'm so demanding," or "I don't deserve this until I do X." This is normal. Your system is trying to protect you by saying, "Hey, let's prepare for disappointment." Over time, as you practice articulating these needs, wants, and optimal dreams, and then go after them, this dynamic can shift.

An affirmation can support this level of self-authorship and alignment in your life. Examples include:

- "I am entitled to a life that honors my wants and dreams."
- "By asking for what I need and want, I'm modeling this practice for my child."
- "Articulating my needs brings more joy to my life."

Identify an affirmation statement that resonates for you or lands as true in your body. This can become your mantra as you continue to uplevel your aligned life. Imagine how your relationship with yourself will grow.

—— "

You are worthy and entitled to *ask* for your dreams.

—— "

In the following exercise, you will identify your specific needs, wants, and optimal dreams. Then you will commit to actions in at least a few of these domains.

EXERCISE > CLAIM YOUR NEEDS, WANTS, AND DREAMS

For *each* domain of life in the following list, consider your minimum viable need, your want, and your optimal dream. Remember to tap into the physical sensations of each level, as you identified in the previous exercise. This will support you to clarify and claim each of the levels.

- Social connection
- Health and wellness
- Creativity
- Learning
- Spirituality
- Romance/sexuality
- Family
- Friends
- Finance
- Career
- Home
- Any other category that feels important to you

--- EXAMPLE ---

Social connection/friends

NEED
See one friend every other week.

WANT
See two friends per week whom I have a deep connection with. Talk monthly to friends who live far away. Go out to dinner once per month with friends. Have two weekends away per year with friends.

continued

OPTIMAL DREAM

Have a close circle of four to six friends who deeply love and care about me and will support me and cheer me on. Have dinner with friends once per week. Go to a personal development retreat with friends once a year and have two other weekends away with friends. Have a weekly call with friends who live far away.

EXERCISE 〉 CIRCLE UP AND GET ACCOUNTABLE

- Look over your complete list. What jumps out at you? What are you aware of?

- Choose at least *three* domains of life that are most important to you. What action will you take in *each* one to align with your needs, wants, and optimal dreams? Following is a prompt to support you with this, but feel free to make it your own.

- By _____ (insert date), I will_____.
  For accountability, I will_____.

——— **EXAMPLE** ———

Romance/sexuality

By October 29th, I will have a conversation with my partner about wanting to have a date night once a month. For accountability, I will ask my friend Susie to text me on Friday to make sure I do it.

Self-Compassion

Many of us have an atrophied self-compassion muscle. Self-compassion is the practice of treating yourself with kindness, grace, and warmth, irrespective of circumstances. It is a thread that strengthens your relationship with yourself and is a balm for your nervous system that grows your capacity to take on greater challenges in service of existential peace.

Sadly, a fair number of my clients believe at first that the only way to perform and get where they want is through being extraordinarily hard on themselves. I see in them a prior version of myself. I asked one client who felt unseen at work, "Do you ever feel a true sense of belonging and acceptance within yourself?" She peered back at me with blank eyes. "Okay, how about kindness, warmth, a feeling of your own humanity and wholeness? Or that sense that you have your own back?" Her eyebrows rose, her head cocked. I recognized that I needed to slow way down.

"Um, no. Do you?" she asked, her voice full of surprise and bite. I didn't take it personally. I knew I was speaking a language that she'd never been privy to.

"Yes, I do . . . *now*. I had to work on it . . . a lot," I answered with conviction.

Self-compassion presents the opportunity to direct your heart toward yourself: to bathe in the love that you so often bestow on others. That may sound cheesy, but if you can accept the truth of this idea, then transformation awaits. I've walked alongside clients who didn't believe in themselves, whose self-talk dripped with vitriol. With self-compassion, they get unstuck and take on new challenges. They're able to take a stand for their needs and wants. They can build a heartfelt relationship with themselves that deepens all of their other relationships. They become their own home base from which to recharge, gain comfort, and use their renegade spirit to shake up the institutions they lead.

We need to love ourselves out of our comfort zones. Feeling deep self-compassion and giving yourself kindness in the face of failure will not turn you into a lazy, sluggish parasite. Instead, it's akin to being nudged out of the nest by a kind hand you can rely on to pick you up when you fall. I balked at this idea at first, believing that the only way to succeed was being hard on myself. I worried that self-compassion would stall me. I dismissed being kind to myself as silly, weak, and a recipe for trouble. Through the exercises represented in this chapter, as well as yoga and meditation, I have been able to grow my self-compassion muscle— and you can too!

EXERCISE 〉 STRENGTHEN SELF-COMPASSION

There are numerous ways to cultivate self-compassion and self-love, and I've seen many of them work very well. Different methods resonate with different people, so experiment with the following exercises. Leave the ones that don't resonate, without a lick of self-judgment.

- Take yourself into nature, somewhere beautiful. Allow yourself to feel the space between you and nature dissolve as a sense of love, acceptance, and beauty fills you. You are made of the stuff of oceans, trees, rivers, and meadows. You are perfectly you. There's no need for you to do anything or be anything in particular. Let the sensations of love fill you. This feeling is available to you anytime you wish. Find a picture, a song, or an object that helps you connect with this feeling.

- Stand in front of a mirror and look at yourself for three minutes. Do not look for flaws. Instead, think about what you appreciate about yourself, the kind of person you are, how you love others. Take it all in as you look at yourself. Then close your eyes and

continued

let your body, mind, and heart reside in that. If this is hard, as it is for many of us, start small with ten seconds and build up from there.

- Imagine yourself as a small child having a hard time. Perhaps you're missing a parent, maybe you've taken a little spill, or you're disappointed about something. Picture your adorable little self and all the emotions present in that moment. You didn't do anything wrong or bad. You were just a little child. Send that child your love, compassion, kindness, and gentleness. Notice what it's like to receive that. You can give yourself these same feelings anytime you wish.

- Consider someone or something you love unconditionally. It might be a child, a family member, or a pet. Allow yourself to experience the sensations of love you feel toward them. Then place a hand on your heart and imagine that love coming right back to you and filling up your own heart. Bask in the sensations you experience there.[7]

- Whichever activity you chose, what was the impact on your emotions, heart, and spirit? Journal your answers.

BONUS EXERCISE

After you complete the previous exercise, journal your answers to the following questions:

1. What did you notice physically during these experiences? Pay attention to the sensations inside and out: temperature, tension/

continued

release, zingy feelings, or waves of sensations running through you. Note what happened in your head, neck, shoulders, chest, solar plexus (just below where your rib cage meets), stomach, abdomen, thighs, calves, feet.

2. What thoughts or emotions arose for you?

3. Which practices or actions will you commit to in order to further your self-compassion and self-love work? These might include positive self-talk, writing down your wins each day, looking at yourself in the mirror kindly for a moment each day, caring for your body by using lotion lovingly, listening to a song that evokes self-appreciation, or feeding yourself the healthy food your body craves.

To Change Something about Yourself, Love It First

In Western culture we have a tendency toward self-improvement. You're reading this book, which means you're in this camp, and so am I. There is boundless possibility to discover who you are and shift aspects of yourself that aren't working for you. However, in the rush toward improvements, we can get our approach wrong. We think we can examine an aspect of ourselves for all its faults, shame it, and change it through sheer force of will. Or we try to disavow a part of ourselves and banish it. This almost always backfires. This part of us tends to get louder, stronger, and more resistant in the face of potential extinction.

I often work with clients on their inner critic. One client I can recall had a particularly nasty one. "You can't do anything right," it hollered. "You can try that idea for your business, but you will fail like you always do!" In response, my client backed away from her dream of creating her own business.

"What's an image of your inner critic that comes to mind?" I asked her.

"An annoying little kid tugging on my shirt to get my attention," she responded, smiling, and brightened. This harmless, heartwarming image gave her the space to see her inner critic as separate from herself. Now, she could examine it without shame or alienation and become deeply curious about what it was up to.

Imposter syndrome is a work-oriented version of the inner critic. It is defined as "self-doubt of intellect, skills, or accomplishments among high-achieving individuals."[8] You may wrestle with imposter syndrome more than with a general inner critic that attacks everything you do, who you are, how you look, and all of your traits and skills. Oftentimes the core needs at the center of imposter syndrome are safety, belonging, and achievement/self-actualization, just like a more generalized inner critic. You can use the following exercise to work with imposter syndrome, too.

To take the sting out of your inner critic, it helps to personify it, as in the previous example with my client.[9] Come up with a name and an image that captures this part of yourself: an annoying little kid, a troll, a monster, a strict teacher, a movie villain, and so on. Initially, you likely have an adversarial relationship with this part of yourself, which is no surprise because it has caused enormous suffering. While the natural tendency is to force it away to get more peace, instead you need a compassionate understanding together. With love, you can begin to understand what this part wants for you: usually safety, belonging, and achievement/self-actualization; in sum, a good life. Of course you want it to employ different methods, but you can love its positive intentions for you.

EXERCISE > GET INTIMATE WITH YOUR INNER CRITIC

Start the process of understanding your inner critic by asking the following questions with an air of authentic curiosity—rather than snarkiness.[10] Answer the following questions as your inner critic:

- When did you first show up?

- When do you feel vulnerable or threatened?

- What do you need?

- What makes you feel safe?

- What do you want for me?

- What is your purpose?

- How do you want to be cared for?

You can journal the responses or answer them in quiet contemplation. The key is to answer as if you are embodying the inner critic. In other words, you answer from its perspective, using *I*. For instance, "I first showed up when you were struggling with writing assignments in middle school."

Through a deeper understanding of your inner critic, there's an opportunity for compassion and love. You will see the gifts your inner critic offers, and how it's trying to help you (even though its methods are painful). As you begin to view this part of you as an ally, the self-berating aspects will soften their hold. The peace of your quieted inner landscape becomes yours to enjoy.

Excavate the Shit Pile of Your Own Shame

Shame is a peace serial killer. Can you imagine sitting on a lovely beach and enjoying the sun on your skin while thinking about what a horrible human being you are and the awful things you have done? No! Lasting peace and deep shame are incompatible.

Everyone has shame about some aspects of their personality or actions they've taken. You cannot hate these away. That will keep you stuck in a cycle of shame: You are ashamed about a part of yourself, and then you are ashamed that you are unable to change it. Paradoxically, the more you lean into loving these aspects of yourself and embracing them with curiosity, the more you will understand their connection to your essence, and the less they will control you.

David Bedrick, a therapist and teacher of what he calls "unshaming," uses a novel approach. He encourages us to become deeply intimate with our shame. As an unshaming practice, he asks, "What's it like to be _____ [insert the thing you're ashamed of—e.g., snarky, selfish, angry]?"[11] In getting radically curious, the shamed part of us can begin to trust enough to reveal itself fully. In this revelation we see the magnificence, genius, and fully expressed humanity that has been hidden away beneath a shroud of shame.

To use an example from my own life, when my youngest child was five months old, she rolled off the bed and hit her head on the floor. I had laid her in the middle of the bed and was digging in a suitcase to find her a "cuter" outfit than the one I already had picked out. In moments, she rolled to the edge, hit the wall beside the bed, and landed on the floor. She sobbed, I sobbed, and I have never forgiven myself for being a bad mom and not protecting my baby in that moment.

Bringing deep curiosity, I realize: The part of me that feels ashamed is the part that wants to do right by my children, to protect them, to be ferocious on their behalf. I so appreciate this part of me. The shame softens. And with curiosity rather than judgment about the part that wanted her to look cute, I stay present to wanting the best for my baby, to have others see what I saw in her, to have her be showered with love and attention.* I have so much compassion and grace for this aspect of myself. It's the more tender side of my mama bear persona. For that I'm grateful. Otherwise, I'd occupy a take-no-prisoners stance on behalf of my children with a hardness, combativeness, and inflexibility. From this more nuanced place, I experience much less shame about the whole incident. My heart softens, my body relaxes.

To use another example and drive home this point, I am also a nail-biter. I feel ashamed of how my nails look and my lack of willpower to resist biting my nails. With inquisitiveness, I notice that I bite my nails when I'm bored, and there's intensity to the action itself. My awareness deepens. The moments when I bite my nails flash before me: in a meeting when I can't say what I want, during a tension-filled television show when I feel empathy for the trapped protagonist, and when I experience an antsyness that I can't act on. When I bite my nails, the part of me that's intense, powerful, and bold is being squelched. I'm proud of this part of me: It's the advocate for others, the part that takes an uncompromising stand for my clients to live their best life, the clear-eyed advocate for change in my local school system. It's my fire and spiciness. I love this part of me. When it's held back, nail-biting is my way of managing the trapped energy. This recognition softens my shame and grows my self-compassion.

Notice how digging into the shame with deep curiosity and reverence helped me see the incredible parts of myself that have been buried. There may be aspects of yourself that you still want to shift or change, even once you've lessened your shame. Great! It will be much

---

* As I write this, I also feel shame that I wanted my child to get attention for her looks, given that as a feminist I don't believe this should be so. See the layers of shame? I can do the same shame analysis described previously.

easier to develop new habits and self-understanding without shame blocking the path.

Imagine that shame is a dragon on the road to healing and growth. You can't change without confronting the dragon. And if you try to avoid it, you'll spend your time and energy hiding instead of taking meaningful action toward what you want.

EXERCISE ⟩ FACE THE DRAGON[12]

Pick something you feel ashamed of and become intensely curious about this part of you. Trust that it has something to offer you: some magic, gift, a longing, a linchpin you've been looking for.

- What is this part of you like? Dig deeply here—what else is it like? How else does it show up? Examine this part from many different angles.

- What does it offer you and the world?

- What would it look like if you honored this part of you more often?

Next-Gen You

We constantly change, but often unintentionally. One client struggled with becoming overwhelmed by her five young children. She reflected on a moment at Costco when she kept her cool as her kid had a tantrum on the floor. "The old me would have been reactive and aggressive, but not anymore." The "old me" in question was herself just two months before—that's how fast we can change, intentionally.

We have been evolving and adapting for billions of years—it's why we are still around. You are not stuck in the way your life has been or who you have been. The next version of you has so much possibility. Your brain is built for constant change, growth, and learning. It's called neuroplasticity. When you have a new thought, perspective, habit, or develop a new skill, your brain changes. You weren't meant to stagnate. In fact, the discontent that arises when you feel stuck in life, have repeating thought-loops, or see yourself being limited at work or in relationships is an irritant that signals stagnation. And that discontent can motivate transformative change.

Although we were designed to thrive on novelty and growth, for many of us that growth is accidental. We encounter a novel circumstance like a new job or a challenging relationship or a setback, and we grow as we navigate it. This is great! *And* you don't have to wait for a new circumstance to spur growth. Rather, you can reinvent yourself based on the future you want to create and who you are yearning to become.

> **"**
>
> ## You can reinvent yourself based on the future you want to create and who you are yearning to become.
>
> **"**

Richard Boyatzis is a psychologist, researcher, and expert in individual and organizational change. He references the "ideal self," which comprises notions of our core identity, aspirations, purpose, hope, and other components of identity, such as values. He distinguishes this from the "ought self," who we think we are *supposed* to be based on others' expectations and beliefs rather than our own. His research has found that this ideal self is a highly effective catalyst for change.[13]

I boil this concept down simply: Who is Next-Gen You? This is an opportunity to identify who you've always wanted to be without the limits of present circumstances, limiting beliefs and mindsets, and others' views of your life defined by their own shoulds, musts, and can'ts. Ask yourself right now: "Who am I ready to become?" Allow yourself to dream just for a moment. There are no limits, barriers, or rules.

Reinvention is probably a misnomer here. In fact, what we are really doing is peeling off the layers that obscure you so that you can become more and more yourself, back to your essence—just like the Golden Buddha.

There is a particular resistance that can show up when we articulate our Next-Gen self. It sounds like:

- "I want to get up early and meditate every day, but I'm not the kind of person who gets up early."

- "I want to be honest with my friends, family, and husband about my needs, but I'm not the kind of person who stands up for myself."

- "I want to have plants in my house, but I don't have a green thumb."

Yet, once you start to *do the thing*—get up, articulate your needs, get some plants—then you *become* that person.[14] You might think that you'll magically become a different person first, but you'll become that person through the actions you take, the state of being you show up with, and the habits you create.[15] Each small step builds on itself with compounding impact. Every time you get up early, it becomes easier the next time, and those few minutes of meditating quickly add up. By the fiftieth time you wake up early, you'll be like my client and refer to your "old self" who slept late and wasn't a meditator.

A second way to develop the awareness of Next-Gen You is Jack Canfield's idea to "act as if."[16] In other words, adopt the quality of being you'd have and the actions you'd take if you were already where you wanted to be. For example, if Next-Gen You writes regularly, then you carry yourself, dress, act, think, speak, and write as if you were that person already. Canfield even references participating in a party in which everyone came as themselves five years in the future. The whole time, they acted "as if"—they were living their future vision.

This is somewhat different from the advice to "fake it 'til you make it." When you're "acting as if," you're experiencing firsthand the felt sense, thoughts, actions, and quality of being of Next-Gen You. You're locking in the imprint of who you want to become. You're not faking anything.

Finally, building a relationship with your future self helps you care more about the consequences of your present choices and actions. For example, if you were deeply connected to and invested in your eighty-year-old self, exercising now would be a no-brainer because you'd want them to be healthy and strong. You have already set up your future self in small ways: you change the toilet paper roll, go to bed at a reasonable hour, and buy health insurance. You can employ this same approach across different domains of your life and with more consequential decisions and actions. Consider that your actions today affect the you of tomorrow.

EXERCISE > VISUALIZE NEXT-GEN YOU

Go to my website, www.therootedrenegade/resources, for an audio version of this visualization.

Create a contemplative setting for yourself by lighting a candle, having a cup of tea, or doing anything else that engenders that state in you.

continued

Allow yourself to settle in. Take some calming breaths. Use your journal to visualize what Next-Gen You looks like five years from now. Include the following to seed specificity and clarity, and add any other details that come to you. The more visual and specific the better.

- How you spend your time

- The relationships that are most satisfying to you

- The strengths and genius you use regularly

- Your relationship with yourself

- Ways you contribute to your community

- The values you live by

- What you do for work

- Ways you honor your legacy

- The qualities you exhibit when you're at your best

- The energy you bring when you walk into a room

- Your impact on those around you

How does Next-Gen You feel in your body? What's your posture? How do you walk? What internal sensations are you aware of?

Make a commitment to implement changes toward Next-Gen You. And get some support from a friend, coach, therapist, partner, or community. Imagine how powerfully you will generate your own peace with this version of yourself operating in the world.

Takeaways: Chapter Seven

✓ A **life map** is a visual representation of your life's journey. This supports you to witness the breadth of your experiences, maintain a broader perspective amid day-to-day life, and spot repeating patterns and themes.

✓ Everyone has **a true essence** deep inside that is often crudded over by experiences and messages that pressure us to stay small and safe.

✓ You can connect with **the voice of your true essence**. It's the voice that says, "This is what you're meant to do"; "You know"; "You are loved."

✓ Certain places offer **a direct route to your essence**. Regularly noticing how you feel in these places creates the muscle memory needed to access your essence. For many people, that place is in nature. Connecting with and listening to your essence regularly can help you access wisdom and internal peace.

✓ Everyone has an **inner pit crew**—a constellation of personality facets that specialize in different qualities of being. The more you understand your different pit crew members, the more strategically you can call upon them for support.

✓ **Maslow's hierarchy of needs** states that certain needs (food, shelter, sleep) are more foundational than others (achievement, creativity). These foundational needs must be met before the higher-order needs can take priority. Stress interrupts this natural order, creating tension as we neglect our foundational needs in service of work, and so on. This is surviving, not thriving.

✓ For each domain of your life, there are three states of satisfaction you will encounter: **minimum viable need**, **want**, and **optimal dream**. By identifying your standards for each of these degrees of satisfaction, you will start down the path of advocating for your own needs, having them met, and raising your expectations for an authentic life.

✓ You cannot change **aspects of yourself that you are ashamed of** through sheer force of will. These parts tend to get louder, stronger, and more resistant in the face of potential extinction.

✓ **Unshaming** is a process by which you can learn to see things about yourself that usually trigger shame—habits, behaviors, and even one-time events—with more self-awareness and insight. With curiosity rather than judgment, you will be able to welcome these parts of yourself.

✓ When you have a new thought, perspective, habit, or develop a new skill, **your brain changes**. Literally. Because you are made for constant change, growth, and learning, self-evolution is a given, and stagnation causes suffering.

✓ **Self-compassion** is the practice of treating yourself with kindness, grace, and warmth, irrespective of circumstances. Without self-compassion, the prospect of failure and its attendant self-beratement is too frightening to risk, so you remain stuck in your comfort zone where growth is impossible.

✓ **Next-Gen You**—the next evolution of yourself: You can begin to identify the next iteration of yourself through insight and small actions that align with your core identity. Your actions reinforce who you are ready to become. And forging a deep connection with your future self clarifies the long-term implications of short-term choices.

Chapter Eight

DEEPEN YOUR RELATIONSHIPS WITH OTHERS

We are currently facing an epidemic of loneliness, which has wide-reaching impacts for physical and mental health, productivity, and happiness.[1] We are inherently social beings, so our relationships are vital to fulfillment and peace. Consider how you feel spending time with people whose company you delight in versus time with those who suck you dry. If you had the choice, you'd likely double down on the former and ditch the latter. Doing so would pay massive dividends to the quality of your life. Like rewiring your relationship with yourself, exploring and enhancing your relationships with others opens up time, space, and energy to enjoy life on your own terms.

Who Drives You Nuts?

There are some relationships in which our differences evoke curiosity, wonder, appreciation, and/or learning. On the other hand, we all have people in our lives who challenge us, confront us, and bring out our worst. These types of relationships are the pebbles in the shoe of peace. The challenge comes when we don't know why it's so difficult to be around them. Understanding this deepens our self-awareness and unearths ways to improve all of our relationships.

Sometimes these folks act in ways that conflict with our values, which causes us friction: the uncle at Thanksgiving who spouts beliefs that are antithetical to our own, the friend who acts in a hypocritical manner that bumps against our values of transparency, or the coworker who seeks out public praise over private pride. Conversely, perhaps *you* feel guilty about dishonoring a value that's important to you, and the "difficult" person easily expresses that value. This guilt comes out sideways as aggravation.

Other times, these "challenging" individuals embody a part of yourself that you're ashamed of. For example, there's a coach whom I follow on social media and whom I really respect but who also is too much for me sometimes—too out there, too in your face, and too edgy. When I'm honest with myself, I realize that I'm ashamed of my own boldness at times because it makes others uncomfortable. Of course, seeing that quality in someone else stirs up angst in me.

These "difficult" individuals might also represent aspects of yourself that you haven't expressed in a long time. Perhaps you were an incredible artist as a kid, but as a busy adult, you forgot that you love to make art. When your friend becomes a successful artist, that may cause tension in your relationship because of your displeasure with your own choices. This breeds envy. When *you* are envious of someone *else*, you long to be how they are, or have what they have, or accomplish what they have.[2] Envy is often the first blush of a longing or dream you have yet to acknowledge to yourself.

Envy seeds relational tension whether you are the originator or the recipient of it. If envy is directed at you, you may conceal an aspect of yourself so as not to invite discomfort or negativity from another person. This can ostracize you from yourself. It can be painful to be in a relationship when envy is the third wheel. Once you realize where it comes from, envy can loosen its hold on you, whether you are the originator or recipient of it.

Finally, you may not have clearly articulated or enforced your boundaries. This causes a relationship breakdown and leads to resentment, annoyance, and the like. Notice the opportunity here to stand firmly and kindly in your boundaries and take space if the other person continually dishonors your boundaries. See the section Creating Beautiful Boundaries on page 168 for more on boundaries.

EXERCISE > IDENTIFY YOUR TENDER SPOTS

Journal your responses to the following prompts:

1. Make a list of the people who make you crazy, aggravated, frustrated, disappointed.

2. From a place of deep curiosity (and belief that there's nothing wrong or bad about the other person), ask yourself: "What are the tender parts in me that each person evokes? What can I learn by navigating this relationship?"

Dealing with Crap Slingers

My mother is deep in the throes of Alzheimer's disease. Several times per week recently, she's been upset with me for leaving without saying goodbye, when I haven't visited in the first place. Other times, she's angry that I beat someone up (or a few people). And still other times, she thinks I've hidden away my children from her. I know I haven't done any of this; it's merely a projection of her own reality and a man-ifestation of her deteriorating brain. I can apologize, honor how she feels, and soothe her without becoming trapped in my own stubborn-ness and righteousness.

Normally, other people's projections are not this obvious. It's a snide remark, criticism, an offhand "I wish you were like . . ." or "Why can't you do . . ." Many of my clients internalize others' criticism by default. I get it because I have struggled with that for much of my life. Criticism began having less of a hold on me when I realized that it's usually more about the other person, and I can decide how much I take in.[3]

Consider rereading the previous section, Who Drives You Nuts? on page 163, from the perspective that *you* may be triggering the crap-slinger, causing them to project on you. This doesn't mean it's your fault. It does mean that you can hold them with compassion and know that projection goes both ways.

Conversely, there are many reasons unrelated to us that can explain why someone is unduly harsh: they are tired, had a fight with their partner, are hungry, are feeling insecure, are stressed, are worrying about someone in their family, are anxious, aren't feeling well, and so on. People vomit their projections and their own context all over us. When I build lists of explanations like these with my clients, they develop a gentler perspective on criticism and learn to take it way less personally.

To drive the point home, I do an exercise with my clients called the Eye Color Critique. Imagine someone criticizes you harshly for your eye color: "Why don't you have blue eyes?" "Your brown eyes are awful. I wish they were blue." "Green eyes, really? Can't you do any-thing about that?" In this context, you would intuitively realize that something is amiss for the other person. What if you allowed yourself the grace to wonder if criticism directed at you has little to do with you at all?

Now, I'm not saying that all criticism is wrong, bad, or unhelpful. Sometimes it's incredibly useful and comes from others wanting the best for you, rather than simply projecting their own garbage. In fact, when I work with clients who think they are "bad" at receiving feedback, they often recognize that not every form of criticism lands destructively. Instead, it matters how the feedback was delivered, the intention of the person delivering the feedback, whether my client feels vulnerable about the subject in question, and whether my client feels empowered to do something about it.

> **"**
>
> **Remember that you are not responsible for other people's feelings, but you are responsible for creating self-honoring boundaries.**
>
> **"**

You get to decide whether you are open to receiving feedback, the boundaries you set for receiving it, if the content is helpful to you, and how to use the feedback. You can support yourself from a place of deep care and ask: "Which part of this feedback feels true to me (even if it's a small percent)? And how do I want to incorporate it so that it's helpful to me?" This is an empowered stance.

Now, a note about nasty folks. If there are people in your life who repeatedly sling shit, you get to decide you're not available for that. *Boundaries, boundaries, boundaries!* Remember that you are not responsible for other people's feelings, but you are responsible for creating self-honoring boundaries.

EXERCISE ⟩ UNDERSTAND HOW CRITICISM WORKS IN YOU

Journal your responses to the following prompts:

1. Describe two times criticism struck you as useful, empowered, or interesting, and two times it felt harsh, unwarranted, or evoked defensiveness in you. Notice the distinctions in context (e.g., tone of voice, where, when, the other person's quality of being, your relationship with the person giving it) and content (what was said) between your different responses to criticism.

2. Based on what you described, what boundaries do you want to create around receiving feedback so that it's helpful to you?

Creating Beautiful Boundaries

Once, when I was working with a client on setting boundaries at her work institution and within her family, she noted, "Boundaries feel so harsh and cold." That perspective maintains the patriarchy, which fails to honor women's needs as full, complete, and worthy. In her many spheres of life—children, friends, extended family, work—my client was running herself ragged and felt like a failure despite her successes. Her own needs, wants, desires, and yearnings were left out in the cold. Creating boundaries felt harsh to her, yet the harshness of her existing quality of life didn't register.

You can spend your whole damn life meeting other people's needs, operating on other people's timelines, and squeezing your own needs into the milliseconds of the day. When you are present to your own mortality, you do not have time for this!

Do any of the following statements sound familiar?

- "Work is a *threat* to my time, but I *have* to be available."

- "I *always* have to be around for my kids or I'm a bad mom."

- "I can't say no or people will be upset."

- "I don't even know what I want or need. I haven't paid attention to that in a long time."

Notice the *musts*, *shoulds*, and *nevers*. This is a disempowered stance that doesn't reflect free will and self-respect. Rather, it's the language of people socialized as women and other marginalized identities who are expected to meet others' needs first, to believe it's "selfish" to advocate for themselves, and to believe that they are responsible for others' actions, emotions, or discomfort (including in the face of their own boundary-setting).

A more generative perspective is that boundaries are your own loving embrace of what matters most to you. Boundaries honor the space and time to do your good work in the world. They train others in how to treat you. They are a full-throated stand for your own self-love and well-being. Boundaries are the invisible demarcation that holds space for your wants, needs, and desires, and they voice what you will not tolerate.[4]

Maintaining boundaries that acknowledge your needs, values, and desire to live on your own terms in service of your legacy can look like:

- "I'm unavailable on that date. I can make it at this time or that."

- "Honey, I'm working right now. I'm happy to play with you when I'm done at 3:00 p.m."

- "It's important to me to balance my work and family time. You can expect a response to email within forty-eight hours on weekdays."

- "When I hear you volunteer me for additional tasks beyond my role, I notice that I feel disappointed because I have a need for fairness. Would you be willing to have a conversation about compensation?"[5]

- "When I see dishes filling the sink, I feel irritated because I have a need for order in our home. Are you willing to wash the dishes you use immediately?"[6]

- "Kids, you're old enough to do your own laundry. Thank you very much."

- "I will not be checking email on vacation, so if you need something from me, please reach out by X date."

If it's hard to identify where boundaries can serve you, examine areas in your life where you feel resentful. Resentment is the consequence of people-pleasing and continually sacrificing your own needs, wants, and dreams. Guilt is the result of socialization that wrongs you for expressing your needs and creating a life-giving relationship with yourself. For the record, taking a stand for yourself in the face of this socialization is countercultural rebellion at its finest. The fact that you feel bad setting a boundary is a signal that you're undermining the capitalistic patriarchy. Your brain will need to hear that again and again because it will feel wrong. Yet, it's completely right on.

As you train yourself to honor your own needs first, ask yourself this question: "If I say *yes*, then what am I saying *no* to?" Conversely, "If I say *no*, then what am I saying *yes* to?"[7] For example:

- If I say *no* to seeing you this evening, then I'm saying *yes* to self-care.

- If I say *yes* to working all weekend, then I'm saying *no* to family time.

- If I say *no* to your emotional venting, then I'm saying *yes* to my well-being.

- If I say *yes* to charging less for my work, then I'm saying *no* to my values of equitable compensation.

Playing with this framework makes the costs of each choice clearer. We sometimes fail to set boundaries because it feels uncomfortable in the moment. Of course it does! But, in essence, you trade short-term discomfort for *long-term* resentment, frustration, and self-criticism; these feel so far off as to be inconsequential in the moment. This yes/no analysis makes the future costs more present in the now.

It's okay if setting boundaries feels uncomfortable at first and if guilt ensues. It's a new way of being in the world and challenging the status quo. You may stumble and feel awkward, and that's perfectly fine. There's an opportunity for self-compassion as you rework your life and relationships to honor your own needs. I promise that in the long term, this initial discomfort is worth it.

A quick note about others' negative reactions to your boundary-setting: When you have weak boundaries, people in your life become accustomed to you saying yes, meeting their needs, having things work for *them*. They expect you will *always* be that way. Our brains want to believe that people's personalities, preferences, and ways of being in the world will be consistent forever because that's predictable and safe.

When you change things up, you can expect others' resistance in the form of criticism, stonewalling, temper tantrums, and the like.

Consider this simply a natural human response to change. Though unpleasant, it doesn't mean you are doing anything bad or wrong. In fact, to put it plainly, you are not responsible for their feelings, nor are you responsible for their poor behavior. They are responsible for their own self-regulation and self-awareness. You will likely need to remind yourself again and again and set another boundary.

As you build your boundary-setting skill, create an arsenal of strategies to support you if discomfort arises. Try identifying the value or priority that you're honoring by setting the boundary (e.g., family, peace, self-care, pleasure, fun, and health). Remind yourself that others' feelings, reactions, and actions are likely a projection of their own issues and have little to do with you. Remember that not honoring your wants and needs leads to stress, resentment, and internalized distress. Note that the momentary discomfort of the conversation is small compared to the long-term impact of letting yourself down. Take exceptional care of yourself (e.g., calming breaths, taking a walk, meditating, getting a massage, asking someone you love to tell you how amazing you are).

EXERCISE ❯ MAKE BOUNDARIES REAL

Journal about the following:

1. Where do I need to set boundaries to honor my own needs? And what do these boundaries look like?

2. What will support me in carrying out these boundaries?

3. What affirmation will reassure me if guilt or discomfort arises after I set a boundary? (E.g., "Honoring my boundaries helps me be there for the people I love"; or "Moms need to take care of themselves

continued

to support their children"; or "I have limited time and energy and I want to save it for things that bring me joy.")

Consider a physical posture that helps you feel safe as you set a boundary. An example is feeling your feet on the floor and straightening your spine and neck.

Which Relationships to Keep and Which to Release

Some relationships fill us up, and others deplete us. If the quality of your life is suboptimal, consider that your relationships may be a place to look for answers. Relationships are a window to knowing yourself, yet we often fall into and out of relationships without intention.

Back in the olden days of human existence, we lived in tribes. Our ability to connect with others, understand and follow the community rules, and belong meant we either lived or died. Our brains are wired to reinforce the importance of social connection. In fact, the parts of our brain circuitry that process physical pain and social pain overlap.[8]

It's clear that we have an intense, primal need to feel connected to people and belong. But does it matter with whom we spend our time? Yes! Of course.

"You are the average of the five people you spend the most time with," says author Jim Rohn.[9] Does this jibe with your experience as you consider who you surround yourself with? If you have kids, consider the five *adults* with whom you spend your time. I have two teenagers, and my average would skew decidedly snarkier if I included them.

We know that moods are contagious, even more so than viruses. It only takes one grumpy person to wreck a meeting. Similarly, a single encounter with a joyous person changes the course of your day. My most recent one was Bob at the wine store in Costco, who upon seeing Worcestershire sauce in my cart, dramatically reenacted its origins for me. What a delight!

Relationships are often the result of circumstance: neighbors, colleagues in abutting cubicles, members of a committee, or parents at the same school. Other relationships are based on roles: daughter, parent, brother, cousin. Neither circumstances nor roles are intentional but are symptomatic of life on autopilot. You can bring greater discernment to whom you spend your time with. Consider choosing people who make you feel seen, understood, and cherished, and who support what you're up to in the world.

Which of the ten people with whom you spend the most time would you choose to begin a relationship with? Notice what comes up if you discover that you wouldn't choose some of them at all. Remember, you have the choice, power, and opportunity to create the relationships that fill you all the way up.

EXERCISE > AUDIT RELATIONSHIPS

1. Make a chart of the ten people you spend the most time with. For each person, list:

   • How they show up (e.g., their most common emotions/ mood states)

   • How you feel when you're with each of them

   • Which qualities or traits you express when you're with them

   • How satisfied you are in this relationship (1–10)

   • One change you could make that would raise your satisfaction

continued

2. Look over your chart. What do you notice? Are there any themes or patterns? What is it like for you being in the relationship you are least satisfied with? Most satisfied with?

3. How would your life change if you took radical action on how you operate in your least satisfying relationships? What changes could you make internally so that you are empowered in all your relationships?

4. What's stopping you from letting go of relationships that don't serve you?

Navigating Relationship Fractures

Many of us are socialized to avoid conflict at all costs and maintain relationships, even when they aren't working. It makes sense given our evolutionary history and our neurobiology, but it doesn't have to be this way. Sometimes relationships are just for a season: college, first jobs, particular life challenges like illness or loss, children's infancy, pandemic pods, a training program. Once the season ends, these relationships can fall out of alignment with our values or interests. Unfortunately, we don't have models or scripts for how to gracefully transition out of relationships that are past their season. As a result, we either continue with an unfulfilling relationship or ghost.

When I was in college, I studied abroad in Spain. I had a long-distance boyfriend from college whom I loved and missed intensely as I was trying to enjoy adventure abroad. Another young woman in my program was in a similar situation. We commiserated often about our heartsickness while we traveled, ate delicious food, navigated challenges in our host families, and attended classes. I thought she would be a lifelong friend. When we returned from Spain to our respective colleges, we talked on the phone and visited each other. Over time, the thread that connected us frayed, and her more challenging personality traits came into greater focus: negativity, argumentativeness, and domination. My own less-attractive personality traits emerged in the relationship as well: righteousness, impatience, and stubbornness. I realized the relationship wasn't serving either of us.

She didn't change and neither did I. Our circumstances did. When she announced that she wanted to join me in California after college, I knew that I had to have a difficult conversation. Ghosting was not aligned with my values.

I told her something to the effect of, "We don't have much in common anymore now that we aren't in Spain." She emphasized our shared memories, so I tried to be clear and kind: "Our friendship isn't working anymore." There were tears for both of us, but that was our last conversation. I call this a *friend divorce*. It isn't pleasant, but it is sometimes necessary.

Ending a relationship isn't the only option when we are not aligned. We can reinvent it, instead, at any time. A friend had a wise therapist who said, "Your old marriage is over. You can decide to create a new one together or leave the relationship, but going back is not an option."

This reinvention perspective is powerful. All relationships have phases with beginnings and endings, but they are often unintentional. We are constantly evolving as individuals, so our relationships must change as well; otherwise, we chafe against the old ways of being together that don't fit our next-gen version. In this chafing, some of us squelch our needs, and resentment takes hold. Others of us leave a relationship in a rupture. The third option is reinventing the relationship from the best of each of us.

Relationship reinvention entails:

- Clarifying the reasons you are in relationship
- Being honest about your needs and creating norms or rules of engagement
- Getting clear about your shared values
- Creating understanding around value differences
- Recognizing and naming the qualities that you want to bring out in one another
- Aligning around how you will navigate conflict

Most of us are unskilled in having these reinvention conversations. We instead fall into default patterns that leave us dissatisfied and hurt. Given this, the practice of reinvention calls for grace and vulnerability. And don't hesitate to get support, whether from a coach, therapist, or a group. There are also many resources available, such as the Nonviolent Communication approach and the Gottman Institute's programs and services.[10] Be bold and seek the support you need.

> **"**
>
> ## Are you open to divorcing yourself, with love, from relationships that don't serve you?
>
> **"**

It takes courage to create relationships that serve you and to stand in the vulnerability of doing so in an openhearted way. So, what's it going to be? Are you ready to surround yourself with the relationships that create an exceptional quality of life for you, even if that requires reinvention? And are you open to divorcing yourself, with love, from relationships that don't serve you?

EXERCISE > REINVENT RELATIONSHIPS

1. Which of your relationships do you want to reinvent?

2. What's your dream for each of these relationships?
   - How do you want to feel in the relationship?
   - Which of your qualities would show up regularly when you are together?
   - What would you be giving to and getting from the relationship?

3. What shifts, actions, or ways of being will support this dream? What will you ask for, and what will you offer? By when?

Transform Your Anger, Fear, and Resentment

Are you holding on to pain with self-righteousness? Do you refuse to give another person the satisfaction of your forgiveness? How's that working for you? I felt like that for a long time. And it was effective in protecting me from pain—until it wasn't.

My introduction to soul-altering forgiveness came from *Ho'opono-pono*, the native Hawaiian forgiveness ritual. I first learned about these practices from *Get Rich, Lucky Bitch! Release Your Money Blocks and Live a First-Class Life* by Denise Duffield-Thomas. I don't love the title, but her work resonates for me.

There are several different *Ho'oponopono* traditions, as the ritual varies from island to island and tradition to tradition, and there are also more secular variations. At their root, all the variations I've seen are about cultivating forgiveness and compassion, releasing the hold of conflicts and grudges, enabling our own healing, and making ourselves right with self and others.[11] In the process of *Ho'oponopono*, you recall the grievance, remember what happened and the emotions associated with the memory, and imagine a conversation with the offender in which you offer forgiveness. There is a mantra associated with this ritual. You say the following to yourself, directed toward the offender: "I love you. I'm sorry. Please forgive me. Thank you." This is an opportunity to take complete responsibility for your life and circumstances.

After my own experience with forgiveness, I created a process that uses the phrasing of *Ho'oponopono* in conjunction with visualization, affirmation, my Reiki practice, the neuroscience of felt experience and embodiment, and the release of energy through physical practices.

I used this process to explore how to forgive my father. He had been diagnosed with ALS (Lou Gehrig's disease) and didn't have many months left. I had spent decades in therapy working through my relationship with him, the harm he'd done to our family, and the estrangement we had in my adulthood. He was a complicated man who dealt with bipolar disorder and narcissism, which had pervaded my youth. He had serial affairs with women close to our family, and he lied when I confronted him about having an affair. In manic states, he was Don Quixote tilting against the windmills of unions, gas car companies, and "liberalism." When he married his mistress after divorcing my mom, he told my sister and me in a parking lot that the deed was done.

In the months leading up to his death, I yearned to make some sort of peace and experience *heartfelt* forgiveness, not the obligatory forgiveness for a dying parent. I wanted to access love, compassion, and tenderness. I understood that he was mentally ill and some of his indiscretions, self-serving, and inability to take others' perspectives resulted from that. But feeling warmth and tenderness was a completely different matter.

Following Duffield-Thomas's process,[12] I wrote down every incident I could remember that I was upset at my dad for—from the tiny moments of frustration or irritation to the large moments that sat like boulders in the middle of my childhood.

The list was more than one hundred items long, scrawled across the pages of my orange journal. For *each* item, I recalled what happened in exquisite detail: the conversation, the time of day, and where we were. I allowed the emotions to come, whatever they were—anger, frustration, irritation, jealousy, sadness, and disappointment. Tears flowed. The emotions moved through me until they were done. Then, I began to speak the words:

"I forgive you—for doing the best you could, for trying, for not knowing how you hurt me. Please forgive me for holding on to my anger, for not seeing you in all your complexity, for not being able to forgive you sooner.

"Thank you—for bringing me into the world, for the time you took with me when I was little, for helping me understand the qualities I wanted in a partner that differ from yours, for helping me know what kind of family I want for my own children, for providing for our family when I was young.

"I'm sorry—that you suffered, that your life was hard, that I've held on to this for so long."

Then I pictured my dad and said, "I love you." I evoked warmth in my heart.

Following that, using my Reiki practice, I connected with where I held the negative memory in my body. I imagined that negative energy as smoke, darkness, heavy stone, sludge, and so on. I inhaled deeply, sending breath and energy to the spot in my gut to dislodge the stuckness. I exhaled, imagining my breath sending the negative energy and heaviness out of me.

After this was done, I moved on to the next item on the list and repeated the process. Over this months-long process, something shifted in me: More of the good parts of my father became visible to me. I was able to recall memories of my early childhood. The angry sludge in my belly loosened.

The final step of my forgiveness ritual is to make a declaration. It could be how you want the relationship to be, how you want to see the other person, how you want to move forward. Mine was: "I appreciate how you were in my early life. I understand that you were limited in what you could offer me, and I hold that with compassion."

When I learned that my father was going into a hospice, it was time to say goodbye. I crafted a letter that shared good memories of him and my deep appreciation for him. I read it to him through the gaps in my sobbing. He couldn't hear well, and his speech was garbled, but I sent him off with the best gift I could give either of us. It was the most connected I'd ever felt to him. Our relationship has strengthened since he's been gone, in part because my wounds have scabbed over without new hurts to reopen them.

Having completed the forgiveness ritual doesn't mean that I have no negative feelings toward my father. I wish that were so, but I am human, so I hold the sore spots with tenderness and remember more of the good parts of his legacy in me.

EXERCISE > FORGE FORGIVENESS

Go to my website, www.therootedrenegade.com/resources, for an audio version of this exercise.

Forgiveness takes time. It can be emotionally raw and tiring. It is crucial to care for yourself as you walk through this. I could only take on one or two memories per day because I would feel drained, get a headache, and experience the flush of energy moving through me, which was exhausting. Drink lots of water and be kind to yourself throughout this. It's okay to go at the pace that feels good for you. We are all different.

continued

1. Call up what happened that you need to forgive if it's a single incident. For multiple incidents with the same person, make a list of events you want to forgive.

2. For each event, be present with the memory, the emotional experience of it, who you were in that moment. Take your time. This is a slow, deliberate process. You can decide how deep you go. For instance, if the memory is too painful, you can decide only to experience it at a level 3 out of 10. That said, if you're able to do so, truly experiencing the emotions can be cathartic.

3. Use the following forgiveness mantras (they are based on *Ho'oponopono*, but the order is different. I have found that this order resonates best for me and my clients; see what resonates most for you):

    • "I forgive you." (Picture saying this to the person in your mind or out loud. Always forgive yourself, too. Say, "I forgive you" to yourself from your deepest essence.)

    • "Thank you" (for the lesson of this moment, for teaching you something about yourself, to yourself for doing your very best).

    • "I'm sorry" (for holding on to this for so long, for blaming yourself, for carrying a grudge against someone else).

    • "I love you" (to yourself, the person who wronged you, a past version of yourself).

    If possible, you want to access compassion when using these forgiveness mantras. With that said, don't fake it. It's okay if you don't feel compassion fully; just try to access it. If it only feels true a little, see if you can grow that feeling.

continued

4. Picture where this memory lives in you—your head, heart, stomach, or other body part. Try to identify the precise spot where it is stored. Then inhale deeply, sending the breath and energy to that area. Exhale it, imagining this memory and all its residual negative energy leaving your body. You might imagine it like smoke or steam or cold leaving you. Do this three times.

   Continue working through all the items on your list, and then move on to step five.

5. Ask yourself, "What's the relationship I want to have with this experience and this person?" This is your new narrative for yourself, and in relation to this person, which will impact the broader arc of your life.

6. Finally, reflect on what your relationship with forgiveness is like now. Are there people and events you aren't ready to forgive yet? What's the cost of holding on to anger and pain, and what's possible if you release that?

---

* Note: Please do not do this exercise with trauma. You'll be remembering these moments in detail, so please get professional assistance before purposely recalling traumatic events. It's important to not retraumatize yourself.

Takeaways: Chapter Eight

- ✓ We all have people in our lives who **challenge us, confront us, and bring out our worst.** The key is to pinpoint why it's so difficult to be around them and what emotions they trigger in you.

- ✓ **Envy** can drive relational tension. Once you realize where it comes from, envy can loosen its hold on you, whether you are the originator or recipient of it.

✓ **Criticism** is usually more about the other person than about you. You get to decide whether you are open to receiving feedback, the boundaries you set for receiving it, if the content is helpful to you, and how to use the feedback.

✓ **Boundaries** honor your free will, your well-being, your own desires, and your own understanding of your limitations. Boundaries preserve the space and time needed to do your good work in the world.

✓ **Resentment** is the consequence of people-pleasing, being unable to tune in to your yearnings, and continually sacrificing your own needs.

✓ While social relationships are important, **not all relationships serve you**. You can choose to prioritize spending time with people who complement you, support you in moving in the direction you're after, and bring out your best qualities.

✓ **Friend divorce** is not pleasant, but it is sometimes necessary in instances where you have fallen out of alignment with a companion.

✓ Sometimes, falling out of alignment in a relationship can be addressed by **reinvention**. This entails clarifying the reasons you are in relationship, being honest about your needs and creating norms or rules of engagement, getting clear about your shared values, creating understanding around value differences, recognizing the qualities that you want to bring out in one another, and identifying ways to manage conflict.

✓ Letting go of anger and resentment toward others can be a deeply healing experience. A **forgiveness ritual** can support you to release anger and allow for new, positive feelings to take its place.

Chapter Nine

DEFINE YOUR RELATIONSHIP WITH THE WORLD

W e often think about relationships in terms of our connections with other humans. However, you are also in relationships with concepts, phenomena, and things.[1] For example, you have a relationship with your home, money, work, time, spirituality, self-care, compassion, the universe, fear, and love. Initially, thinking about relationships this way might seem odd, but as you experiment with this idea, you will notice that it creates entirely new perspectives and greater agency.

To make this relationship lens more concrete, consider: When you ask someone what they *think* about money, you're asking their thoughts about the idea at this finite moment in time. However, if you ask someone about their *relationship* with money, it evokes a nuanced response that takes into consideration mind, body, and emotion. People often drop down into a slower, more self-reflective frame of mind than when you merely ask what they think about something.

The dynamics of a relationship are organic, shifting based on your experiences, context, and level of self-awareness. The mutuality is like a dance between you and the concept. If you allow it to, this relationship lens can spur insights and empower you to create a relationship with the world that serves you.

Examining Your Relationships with Universal Ideas

Let's dig deeper by looking at a couple of concrete examples, starting with hope. My own relationship with hope was born of rife circumstances. I was sixteen weeks pregnant with my first child when I developed excruciating pain that made me vomit and moan. For days. On the third ultrasound, it was finally clear that I had an ovarian torsion, where the ovary twists over on itself, cuts off the blood supply, and dies. I needed emergency surgery. Hope felt like a bated breath—*tentative*. I longed and wished and prayed for my baby and me to be okay. But I also tamped down hope, steadying myself against the possibility of miscarrying during the surgery. At that moment, hope and I did a dance of ambivalence.

After the surgery, I had a small amount of spotting. My heart sprinted during my next ultrasound. I bored my eyes into the image of my baby on the screen. As soon as I heard the reassuring *wsh-wsh-wsh* sound of my baby's heart, hope blossomed into certainty. Now, I have a trusting relationship with hope. I can take it off the shelf, borrow it, bask in it for as long as I need it, and return it when I'm done. I know it will support me and walk with me through harrowing experiences.

But that's just *my* relationship with hope. Other people's relationships with hope may include increased energy, a sense of possibility, a desire to be fully present, fear, or even distrust. These relationships change over time, just as our relationships with people do.

To use another example, consider: What is your relationship with time? Yes, you are in a relationship with time. And even though everyone has the same number of hours in a day, some people feel like it's a one-way relationship in which time acts as a controlling or limiting force.[2] To them, that might feel like:

- "Time is a limited resource. There are twenty-four hours in a day, seven days in a week. Period."

- "I'm up against the clock."
- "I'm at war with the clock."

Others are present to a fluid, subjective relationship with time. Think of the difference in the way you experience time when you are sitting on a beach versus rushing someone to an emergency room. It might be the same thirty minutes, but you will have a vastly different subjective experience.

Still other people may have an expansive relationship with time, in which they feel they can generate whatever time they need. Gay Hendricks points out this relationship with time in his book *The Big Leap*: "Since I'm the producer of time, I can make as much of it as I need!"[3] He rightly says that people blame time rather than owning that something just isn't a priority.

When my clients recognize that they are in a relationship with time, their perspectives loosen, they have more flexibility of thought, and they recognize all the choices before them. They shift their language related to time and build a bridge to the relationship they want to have.

The following are examples of shifting your time-related language to be more empowering:

- "This just isn't a priority for me" instead of "I don't have time."
- "I create the time for the things that matter" instead of "There aren't enough hours in the day."
- "It's how we use the time we have" instead of "We all have the same amount of time."
- "This is just one moment in the infinite expanse of time" instead of "Use every second or lose it."

Again, this relationship lens applies to any concept you want to examine. We internalize the messages we tell ourselves, so ensure that your language aligns with the relationship you want to create with universal concepts. And if you are having the same challenge repeatedly or feel limited in some aspect of your life, ask yourself: "What is the relationship I want to create with [the concept or phenomena causing me trouble]?"

EXERCISE ⟩ EXPLORE YOUR RELATIONSHIPS WITH UNIVERSAL IDEAS

Journal about your current relationship with time, money, love, work, home, envy, pain, spirituality, or anything else that is a persistent challenge area for you. Answer the following questions:

- As you read this journal entry, which insights stand out to you?

- How does this relationship lens create more options in your life?

Blow Your Mind

Most of us have experienced transcendent moments. Perhaps you've felt at one with the universe and with others, or even beyond your material existence. Maybe you have experienced infinite love and acceptance for yourself and all of humanity. Or it's possible that you have looked across a vast expanse in nature and simply known that everything works out as it should. These moments might have occurred in deep meditation, in a natural setting with an otherworldly vista, or during a moment of complete presence that activates all your senses.

Interestingly, these experiences often cause us either to go deep inside ourselves or far outside of us to access new ways of thinking, feeling, or knowing. In fact, research shows that experiences that engender awe "may be one of the fastest and most powerful methods of personal change and growth."[4]

There is a common hue to the thoughts that emerge during these experiences: wisdom, expansiveness, resourcefulness, existentialism, confidence, and groundedness.

And they sound like:

- "The universe has my back."

- "Everything works out for a reason."

- "The universe is expansive, and I'm just a tiny part of it."

- "I'm here for a reason. I want my life to mean something."

- "I have always been here and will continue to always be here, just in different forms."

Yes, these thoughts sound trippy. But most of us have had these thoughts without being under the influence. I consider these thoughts our natural state when everything else is at equilibrium. If you are depleted, mind-blowing thoughts evade you. They are replaced by unhelpful thought-loops that attempt to settle your nervous system back to equilibrium (and fail). You seldom experience these types of thoughts in your day-to-day life in part because modern life operates at odds with your natural, evolutionary preferences: deep connection and movement; natural settings; a slower, restful pace; and deeply felt wisdom.

Given that you probably can't move to a monastery to create a context more aligned with your optimal state, you need to find more accessible ways to connect with these thoughts, feelings, and whole-body experiences. There are two access points. The first is to seek out daily contexts that engender these mind-blowing states: nature, meditation, prayer, stream-of-consciousness writing, flow states, and awe-inducing experiences (in tiny moments and expansive settings).[5] The second access point is to think these thoughts on purpose. If you want to believe *the universe has my back* as your stance toward the world, you think the thought and notice the impact on your feelings, body sensations, and actions. Then remind yourself to think that thought regularly. Nudge yourself to notice examples of when the universe has acted this way: the parking spot that appeared; the time you caught your child from falling; the right-place, right-time meeting of your partner; the new client that miraculously appeared at the right moment; and so on.

You even have a part of the brain that rejects information that is contrary to your beliefs and notices information that supports your beliefs. These brain components are your posterior medial frontal cortex and reticular activating system, if you want to get neuroscience fancy.[6]

EXERCISE > **EMBRACE PERSPECTIVES ON THE WORLD**

Journal your responses to the following prompts:

- What perspective do you want to embrace about the world, the universe, and your place in it? Consider how you want to feel moving through your life.

- What thoughts will you think on purpose related to this perspective, and what structures will support you to make this a regular practice (e.g., journaling, Post-it notes, screen savers, reminders, a mantra before bed or upon waking)?

Takeaways: Chapter Nine

✓ All of us exist in relationships with **ourselves** and **others**, as well as with **concepts, phenomenas, and things.**

✓ Examples of this relationship lens include our relationship with hope and with time. You get to **create the relationship** with these ideas that serves you most by reframing your language and noticing when your experiences align with the relationship you desire.

✓ **Experiences that engender awe** may be one of the fastest and most powerful methods of personal growth and change. But if you are depleted, mind-blowing thoughts will evade you in favor of unhelpful thought-loops focused on trying to get you back to equilibrium. By intentionally seeking out **experiences that encourage mind-blowing thoughts** and training yourself to **think these thoughts on purpose,** you get to **create a relationship with the world that supports your renegade life.**

PART IV

EXPLORE THE PEACE DOJO

You may encounter many defeats, but you must not be defeated.
In fact, it may be necessary to encounter the defeats, so you can know who you are,
what you can rise from, how you can still come out of it.

—MAYA ANGELOU

We must integrate our hardest moments if we are to live as fully expressed humans, rather than hollowed-out ones. The time and energy we spend suppressing our most trying experiences narrow our emotional existence. And fear, avoidance, and shame run the show until we confront these painful moments.

In this section, you'll discover the wisdom and capacity that reside in your most challenging experiences. This realization holds the keys for your transformation. We will also tread new ground in looking at facets of peace we haven't explored yet.

Chapter Ten

LEARN FROM YOUR DARK NIGHT OF THE SOUL

All of us have experienced a dark night of the soul: the moment that follows disaster, failure, death, or illness when hope feels lost, meaninglessness pervades, and our old life is no more.

Author Joseph Campbell wrote prolifically about the "hero's journey" as a concept in literature and across cultures. He outlines the process the hero goes through within myth and notes, "The dark night of the soul comes just before revelation. When everything is lost, and all seems darkness, then comes the new life and all that is needed."[1] It is often a spiritual crisis, a purpose crisis, an existential crisis, a *what the fuck am I doing with my life* crisis.

The Alchemy of Darkness

Dark nights of the soul can catalyze tremendous personal growth and change, shifts in your life trajectory, or reprioritization. I call this transformation the *alchemy of darkness*. We must experience some form of friction to grow, otherwise we'd coast along in the status quo. That doesn't mean you experience joy or appreciation when these dark nights are happening, however. Transformation can feel eviscerating.

But eventually, you will need to face the agony to understand who you are meant to be and what you are meant to express in the world. Without that, you will constantly run from the pain. Only with the space of time and reflection do the offerings of this ugliness come into view.

One of my dark nights of the soul occurred when I was working as a director at a nonprofit organization. Many circumstances contributed to my growing anxiety at the time: confronting a toxic work culture, traveling a lot for work, feeling disconnected from my kids due to the travel, managing an increasing workload, being unable to draw boundaries, my ADHD spinning out of control, and dealing with a chronic health condition. These factors mounted without my awareness of the physical and emotional toll they were taking on me.

Two nights before I was scheduled to give a talk at a conference, my insomnia began. In the hours before my talk, my throat felt like it was closing. I worried that I was having an allergic reaction. As the minutes passed and my presentation drew closer, I started having heart palpitations and began sweating. In the moments before, as I sat offstage, it felt like someone was jackhammering outside. I even peeked out the window. No, it was my own internal shaking. I managed to get onstage, and then I realized that I had to hold the microphone, advance the slides, and turn the pages of my notes. I didn't have enough hands! I tried without the microphone, but the audience couldn't hear. So I stumbled through the presentation, heart pounding, sweating, shaking, and feeling unable to breathe. I felt like the inside of my body was opening and might just swallow me.

My inner monologue screamed in my head: "What the fuck is wrong with you? You're going to be fired! You look like an idiot! More of these presentations are coming. You will die!"

Over the next few weeks, shame consumed me, and my insomnia became intractable. I stumbled around, not realizing the impact of sleeplessness on my chronic illness. I stayed in bed for hours, full of self-loathing. I saw my therapist twice a week. My doctor ignored the severity of the situation, despite my pleas. I tried acupuncture and sleep medications. Nothing helped. My mom came to help with my kids, as I could barely shower or eat. The prospect of additional talks in the future made it impossible to heal, so I left my job. I couldn't even get the words out to explain to my boss what had happened; it was as if humiliation had consumed my voice.

On one particularly bad night, I thrashed around in bed, unable to sleep. The words swirled in my head repeatedly that I was an idiot and a failure, my family was ashamed, I'd never work again, and anxiety would always cripple me. I wanted to claw my skin off and escape. I cried in my husband's arms. "I think I might have to go to the psychiatric hospital," I gulped, sobbing. This was the darkest of many dark nights of the soul. I thought the situation would last forever, that I was doomed and unlovable. I couldn't imagine feeling any other way than I did in that moment.

"If you need to go to the hospital, then I'll take you to the hospital," my husband said, looking at me with devotion and tenderness. In that moment, I loved him more than I could ever love anyone. That he could hear my truth and love me meant that I could heal alongside him. It was the first stitch in repairing the thing that had broken in me. I basked for a moment in the sensation of complete acceptance.

I didn't realize at the time that the insomnia and lack of appetite, combined with a chronic illness that affects my adrenal system's ability to metabolize stress, was a perfect storm of physical and mental distress.

After weeks of medication, therapy, acupuncture, and space from the pressure of work, things finally began to lighten, and I felt myself returning. It was several months before my strength had fully recovered. Through this process, I grew an even deeper appreciation for my husband, and I clung to his security and love as I healed. I would grin in his presence and hang on to his solidity. I had a burst of creative energy and wrote a lot: essays, children's stories, journal entries.

Over the ensuing months, I realized that this dark night of the soul contained many revelations. First, I wasn't well suited to the work I was doing, despite believing in the mission. Next, it was vital to prioritize both my physical and mental health, always. I also saw that aspects of the job compromised my values, such as family and collaboration. Challenging work dynamics had led me to waste my psychic energy. And finally, my husband and I had a special kind of relationship that I vowed to cherish.

This dark night of the soul led me to pursue coaching, which is my soul's work. I didn't want others to walk this same road of burnout, self-recrimination, pain, and stifled humanity and wholeness.

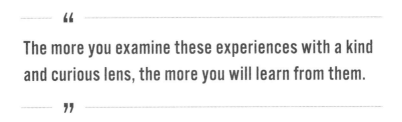

The more you examine these experiences with a kind and curious lens, the more you will learn from them.

Over the six years since that night, I have worked hard to hone my perspective on this event in the grand scheme of my life. I examined what this experience made possible for me and what I learned about myself. Because of this, I can connect with gratitude for my crash-and-burn moment and recognize it as the gift it was. Yet, it still contains a kernel of shame: feeling weaker than I consider myself to be; being unable to care for my kids for a couple of weeks; and leaving my job abruptly in a manner that felt out of alignment with my values of honesty and respect. When these feelings come up, I try to speak to myself with grace, love, and self-compassion. And I repeat the unshaming process from Chapter Seven, Excavate the Shit Pile of Your Own Shame on page 154.

Integrating Your Dark Night of the Soul

In myself and my clients, I've seen a dynamic in which our shame prevents us from mining the revelations contained within our suffering and failures. This keeps the pain present and growth at bay. The more you examine these experiences with a kind and curious lens, the more you will learn from them. Otherwise, it's all for naught—pain but no gain.

Without integrating these experiences, you might limit your emotional and experiential range. To blunt the tough emotions of these experiences, you may disconnect from all your emotions. You might even avoid situations that are reminiscent of your dark night of the soul and resist looking at your past. With support, you may realize that you are exhausted and have become a shell of your former self. The mental energy needed to avoid and temper your emotions—even as you long for the full expression of your humanity through your emotions—leaves you hollow. That's when integration and seeing the gifts of these experiences can unfold.

The following exercise is intended to help you gain a new perspective on your dark night of the soul. Only you can decide how deeply you want to delve into this exercise and what support you might need. You may wish to skip the narrative reframe part of the exercise and just journal responses to the bulleted questions in number five. If any of your dark nights are traumatic, please get support from a therapist to work on the trauma and skip this exercise. It can be triggering to dive into these memories.

EXERCISE ❯ MINE YOUR DARK NIGHT OF THE SOUL

Many of us have more than one dark night of the soul. Examine the span of your life in the following age brackets, and jot down briefly any dark nights of the soul within them. Once you have listed your dark nights of the soul, you'll write about one at a time following the steps after the age bracket list. Go through all the following steps for each dark night of the soul before you move on to the next.

Ages

- 0–5
- 6–12
- 13–18
- 19–26
- 27–39
- 40–60
- 61–80
- 81–100

1. Select a dark night of the soul and write what happened as a reporter might—factually. Try as best you can to excise the emotions. There are, of course, many emotions in our dark nights of the soul; we'll get to these in the next step. Write in the third person.

   Example: "Rebecca walked up to the stage. She fumbled with the microphone and slides. She spoke in staccato . . ."

   You are practicing distance and cultivating your observer qualities. You are also getting as clear as you can on the facts. Remember: Do this for one dark night of the soul first.

2. Now rewrite the narrative, including the facts as in step one AND any emotions that were present.

   Example: "Rebecca walked up to the stage. She was nervous and apprehensive. She fumbled with the microphone and slides and was overwhelmed . . ." Do this for the same dark night of the soul as in step one.

continued

3. Now rewrite what happened with complete self-compassion,[*] as if you were writing about a friend's or child's experience. Infuse the narrative with self-love and grace, including facts, emotions, context, and anything else that feels true and important.

"Rebecca was so nervous walking to the stage—of course! It was her first talk in a long time, the audience was large, and her boss had high expectations and demands. She had done her best to prepare but didn't realize how nervous she would be in the moment. It's so common for people to be nervous about public speaking. How could they not have a microphone stand? No one can be expected to hold a microphone, advance the slides, and work with their notes at the same time. Why didn't the organizers think of this? She did the best she could to remember what her boss had said and to manage the clusterfuck of technology . . ."

4. Write one more version, this time from the first person ("I") perspective.

"I was so nervous walking to the stage—of course! It was my first talk in a long time, the audience was large, and my boss peppered me with things I had to remember to say. I had done my best to prepare—staying up late, reworking slides, reviewing my notes, practicing—but I didn't realize how nervous I would be in the moment . . ."

5. Read over the last narrative and answer the following prompts:

- What opportunity has your dark night of the soul given you for growth and learning? A changed trajectory? A different relationship with yourself, others, the world?
- What are you grateful to yourself for as a result of this experience?

continued

- How will you support yourself to forgive anything that remains to be forgiven?

6. Repeat this exercise with as many dark nights as you want. Ensure that you are taking exceptional care of your physical and mental self during these exercises. Examples include having a lovely cup of tea, lighting a candle, carving out time and space, getting a massage—whatever you do that helps you feel loved, cared for, restored, and peaceful.

---

* Note: It's often hard for us to access self-compassion when our inner critic runs the show. It's helpful to reframe by considering how you would speak to a small child who made a mistake or was having a hard time: "Oh, honey. It's okay. Everyone makes mistakes sometimes." "You did your best. You aren't a bad person." "I love you, and you are okay." Can you speak to yourself with the same love, care, and tenderness as you recount your dark night of the soul? Reread the section in Chapter Seven, Self-Compassion on page 148 if you need a reminder.

Takeaways: Chapter Ten

✓ The **dark night of the soul** comes just before revelation. It can catalyze tremendous personal growth and change, a shift in your life trajectory, or reprioritization.

✓ Holding on to shame about your dark nights of the soul leaves you **unable** to **mine the revelations contained within your toughest moments.** You limit your emotional and experiential range when you cannot integrate these experiences.

✓ **Self-compassion** is the key to softening shame and allowing yourself to access the insights offered by dark nights of the soul.

Chapter Eleven

UNCOVER WHAT REMAINS

We've been down a long path together exploring many aspects of rooted peace and life lived on your own terms. In the previous chapters, you delved into the content I have found is most crucial for my clients and myself on this journey. With that said, I'd be remiss in talking about peace without including some of the concepts that follow. This chapter features a compilation of not-to-miss peace concepts designed to point you in the direction of different areas to explore on your own, to question, to shake loose, and to sink into.

Rooted Peace Is . . . Empowered Spirituality

Many people turn to spirituality and religion to cultivate a sense of peace and surrender. In numerous religious traditions, there are practices that evoke peace—whether through prayer, ritual, beliefs, texts, or songs. Consider the calming experience of lighting candles, entering a place of worship, hearing a particular prayer or text, or feeling that a loving presence watches over you. These elements often create an embodied sense of peace and support.

In my home, we integrate cultural traditions of Judaism and Christianity loosely, to say the least, and often irreverently. The rituals, particularly Passover, create a thread that connects us to a larger story of our ancestors far and near. Our Haggadah (guide for the Passover ritual) is a family heirloom—not the expensive kind, but a deeply treasured one. It's my hilarious grandfather's typewritten pages that yield an efficient run-through of the ritual. The names of parts played by long-deceased family members fill the margins. As I glide my hand across the page, I feel myself connecting with all of them and with Passovers long since past. A peace washes over me knowing that I was loved and held by these people. This is the point of religious traditions, I believe.

When you look across traditions, there are many commonalities in beliefs and practices that generate a warm and loving relationship between the individual and God/spirit/higher power/humanity. These commonalities seem divinely inspired—or at the very least, deeply informed about ways to evoke the best of human nature.

Spirituality is a deeply personal journey. When I work with clients who are wrestling with aspects of their faith traditions, I approach the issue with humility. I've seen spirituality be a tremendous support for some clients and a cause of suffering for others. During our work together, my clients often land on the notion that spirituality can be a choice, rather than something imposed on them.

You can choose to lean into the beliefs and practices that center your humanity, support you in asking the big questions, and connect you with something larger than yourself—or whatever aspects of spirituality resonate for you. The point is self-authoring your own spirituality as a place to come back to again and again and draw strength from, rather than something to fear, avoid, and manage.

You may find as you've worked through this book that you are stripping away the layers of ego, unhelpful coping mechanisms, shame, and people-pleasing. In their place is connection to your truest essence, deepest longings, and intuition. Don't be surprised if you have easier access to spirituality as a result.

Consider how you want to draw from your religious traditions or explore your own spirituality to purposefully create greater love, connection, meaning, and support.

Rooted Peace Is . . . Using Disruption as a Tool for Healing

We carry many narratives about disruption or conflict: It's bad and wrong; it's disempowering; it's unsafe; it's to be avoided at all costs; it undermines peace and love. These ideas often come from witnessing others' unskillful or even scary ways of dealing with conflict. However, disruption has the potential to heal and deepen our relationship with ourselves, others, and the world.

Consider how your dark night of the soul was a disruption to the status quo of your life that catalyzed learning, transformation, and even a new life trajectory. This breach was necessary to break you out of the lull of day-to-day existence. The consequence was a deeper relationship with yourself that carries forth for the duration of your life. There is so much power and possibility within disruption.

Conflict with others makes conscious and visible what otherwise operates below the surface. Have you ever sat with long-simmering emotions such as resentment, disappointment, and frustration? I have! When my kids were little, I'd stuff down my feelings of resentment about carrying too much of the mental load for our home and our kids. I'd stifle feelings of disappointment about my husband not taking ownership of his share of the tasks. I'd squash frustration that our house was a mess, and I was the only one doing anything about it. This suppression didn't mean that conflict was absent. Instead, it was merely unspoken. I had many imaginary conversations with my husband: I'd come up with retorts, I'd gather evidence of his failings, and

I'd judge his choices. This did not create peace for me or for him, even if conflict simmered below the surface.

"

If you embrace and welcome disruption, it enables you to create something different.

"

Once my pressure cooker of squashed emotions boiled over, disruption unfolded. I'd yell and cry and issue my proclamation of grievances. Even this unskillful conflict was better than trying to contain it. It gave my husband and me a chance to view the circumstances, voice our feelings, correct misunderstandings, and take responsibility. We were able to decide how we wanted our home to operate and how to occupy our different roles within it. Did we handle it perfectly? *Hell no.* But there was liberation in voicing my suffering.

If you embrace and welcome disruption, it enables you to create something different. As you practice having regular conflict and no longer fearing it, you will gain greater comfort voicing your discomforts, hurt feelings, needs, and desires. From that place, you will come into deeper relationship with yourself and others. Peace and healing unfold from this connection and space of co-creating possibilities for your life, rather than using energy for avoidance.[1]

Disruption is the compost for healing in our world at large, too. Christiana Figueres, executive secretary of the United Nations Framework Convention on Climate Change from 2010 to 2016, was instrumental in crafting the Paris Agreement on climate change. She notes: "Climate change is the gym in which we as human beings are strengthening our muscle to be able to evolve to a much higher sense of awareness, consciousness, action than we were before."[2]

There's so much disruption needed in the world right now, in service of healing from what's already broken. Don't be afraid to lean into the power of disruption to forge a future that works for all of us. What can be your renegade role in this?

Rooted Peace Is . . . Irrespective of Circumstance

We have covered many ways to shift your environment to support greater peace: being in nature, imagining yourself in the places that directly connect you to your essence, tapping into the environments in which you feel most spacious and calm. And yet, we have all experienced moments when the environment and circumstances were optimal, but peace evaded us. For example:

- You go out to a lovely dinner and can focus only on the sound of the air conditioner.
- You sit by a lovely lake and think about a conflict you are avoiding.
- You snuggle under a warm blanket but feel isolated from your friends.

Conversely, you've likely also had moments that felt serene even amid utter chaos:

- You laugh at the ridiculousness of your toddler sprawled out in the grocery store aisle.
- You catch the sunset in the middle of a traffic jam.

- You find yourself focusing on your husband's sparkling eyes in the middle of a heated discussion.

This is a powerful recognition because you don't *have to* change your context to create the peace you deserve. You can generate the circumstances that make peace *more likely*, but if you don't manage your internal experiences alongside that, the circumstances are less relevant. Sure, attend to your external circumstances, but more importantly, attend to your inner experience—the thoughts, ideas, and body sensations that generate the experience of peace you're after.

Rooted Peace Is . . . Free, but the Absence of Peace Is Expensive

Consider the actual financial costs of generating peace within yourself—nothing. Now, consider the lengths you go to when you don't have peace: booking expensive vacations to escape from life; endless buying to achieve the high of consumerism; bingeing on social media, food, alcohol, and drugs for momentary bliss and escape; wasting time, attention, health, and energy. What's the total amount of these costs, for the whole country? Billions, I'll bet.

Consistently generating internal peace, existential peace, and relational peace through your conscious choices is free—and it's priceless.

Rooted Peace Is . . . Surrender

I have never liked the word *surrender*. I'm a New Yorker by birth. I like to make stuff happen, to advocate for myself and others, to fight against inertia, and "control the crap out of things," as my own coach likes to say. Surrender always seemed like a cop-out, in the same way that destiny feels like absolving oneself from the responsibilities of free will. If I were to surrender, wouldn't that yield complacency, passivity, and a tuned-down life with less motivation and joy? No. Surrender is an act of choice, power, intention. It's deciding on purpose to release what you can't control instead of deluding yourself into thinking that with enough force of will, you can.

> "
>
> **When you release the fist of control, you get to enjoy more and be present with what is, instead of wishing for something else.**
>
> "

When I was a kid, my dad had a mix tape with the song "Secret Garden" by Carol McComb. It shared the truism that the tighter you grip something, the less that remains. My ten-year-old brain turned that over repeatedly.

This is what surrender is like. When you release the fist of control, you get to enjoy more and be present with what is, instead of wishing for something else. You create a clearing for intentionality instead of frenetic action. You lessen the emotional turmoil of anxiety. And you drop into a spaciousness that sources you, instead of a control that sucks you dry. From this place we have so much autonomy and calm.

Rooted Peace Is . . . Embracing Paradox

Our brains resist paradox. They will examine a paradox from every angle, hoping to find one where it makes sense. And yet, there is so much wisdom in the paradoxes that surround us, particularly those related to peace. They are meaty concepts to contemplate or to let simply wash over you. Allow yourself a little space to let each of the following paradoxes into your system and see what unfolds.

Aesop's fable "The Tortoise and the Hare" demonstrates the paradox "go slow to go fast" when the slow, plotting tortoise beats the fast, frenetic, and arrogant hare. If you try to move faster and faster in your work, you make more errors, bring less intention, and end up duplicating efforts or failing to use your resources strategically. Alternatively, if you take step-by-tiptoed-step, you will make steady progress, build momentum and confidence, and generally feel more grounded and confident as you go. Hence, it becomes a peaceful process instead of a handwringing one. The next time you have a project at work or at home, consider going slow to go fast, and enjoy the process more.

Some of my very busy, high-achieving clients resist well-being routines like exercise, meditation, or a hobby they love. "I have no time!" they exclaim. I get it. We are trained in blaming time for things we aren't ready to claim as a priority. But they would do well to reflect on the paradox "spend time to get time." Why? For the same reason that busy CEOs like Arianna Huffington, Oprah Winfrey, Bill Gates, and Jeff Weiner of LinkedIn all meditate often, even though they have tons of demands on their time. Meditation creates more thoughtfulness, creativity, and emotional bandwidth. Spending half an hour meditating means wasting less time scurrying around like a headless chicken, less time ruminating, and more time being tuned in to the true priorities. They make up the time they spend meditating and then some. If Oprah can do it, so can we!

Similarly, consider how good you feel after you exercise. You have more energy, drive, enthusiasm, and capacity. Imagine how much you could get done diving into your day from that energetic space—and how you'd feel while doing it. It's radically different from the slow-roll slog: get coffee, open computer, check social media, waste time on email, look at calendar and fret about what's coming up, and write out a to-do list in slow motion to avoid having to start it. To uplevel your quality of life, try carving out time for self-care and see how much more time you create.

More generally, start to notice what it's like to hold paradoxes in your consciousness without trying to have them make sense or fit. Being able to sit with opposing ideas simultaneously and easefully is a superpower in navigating the complexities of life. Which other paradoxes are you aware of related to internal, existential, or relational peace?

Rooted Peace Is ... Yours, Even If

Peace is yours, even if your sink is full of dirty dishes, you didn't finish your to-do list, you swear, you turn your underwear inside out when you haven't done laundry, you're angry and judgy, or irreverent, and so on.

None of us is perfect. Without harsh self-judgment, would it matter that your sink is full, your to-do list isn't done, and you swear? No. There's no final arbiter of whether your life has been well used other than *you*.

Rooted peace is your birthright. You don't have to earn it. It's a common human experience to seek peace. It's so readily available to you through your breath, it seems part of the default settings of the human operating system. Peace is the result of the choices you make. You don't have to deserve it or find it in external sources. It's all simply you.

Rooted Peace Is ... Strong Back, Soft Front

If you are a direct, bold individual who says it like it is and isn't afraid to stir things up, you can still be a rooted renegade. Standing in your capacity to create peace for yourself does *not* mean being meek, quieting your voice, or being "nice." Those, in fact, are acts of violence against yourself, using your energy for self-suppression. You hold back your essence, edit your words and emotions, and contain and constrict your body. You wither under these conditions, so it's no surprise you get gunked up. The energy that is suppressed must go somewhere, so it turns against you.

Imagine, instead, simply letting your boldness be released into the world, naming what you see and feel unapologetically, offering your genius with confidence, and giving other people the opportunity to truly know you and see you. In doing so, you become your own self-actualizing, ass-kicking savior.

Of course, I'm not saying that in leaning into your boldness you should be nasty to other people. "Strong back, soft front" is a concept coined by the Zen teacher Roshi Joan Halifax. It means you can have confidence and strength alongside an openhearted gentleness. This is not a paradox, as each makes the other possible. False confidence can lead to hardened self-righteousness rather than softness—and without the support of a strong back, you will fail to honor your own needs, can be taken advantage of, and can end up depleted and hostile.

Takeaways: Chapter Eleven

- ✓ You can choose to **lean into the spiritual beliefs and practices** that center your humanity, support you in asking the big questions, and connect you with something larger than yourself—or whatever aspects of spirituality resonate for you.

- ✓ **Disruption** has the potential to heal and deepen your relationship with yourself and others. If you embrace and welcome conflict, it enables you to co-create something different.

✓ You can generate the circumstances that make peace more likely, but if you don't manage your **internal experiences** alongside that, you will not succeed.

✓ Consistently generating internal peace, existential peace, and relational peace through your conscious choices is free—and it's priceless. The **price you will pay to achieve momentary happiness** by other means—vacations, food, conspicuous consumerism—is far higher.

✓ **Surrender** is deciding on purpose to let go of things you can't control instead of deluding yourself into thinking that with enough force of will, you can. From a place of surrender you can find so much autonomy and calm.

✓ **Paradoxes** can deliver valuable insight: "go fast to go slow"; "spend time to get time." Try sitting with different paradoxes as a practice to support you in managing the complexities of life. Allow your brain to turn them over and see what realizations unfold.

✓ **Rooted peace is your birthright.** You don't have to earn it. *You* are the only final arbiter of whether your life has been well used.

Conclusion

YOU'RE A ROOTED RENEGADE NOW

The pandemic brought immense tragedy and suffering. Seven million people died. And yet, you survived that collective near-death experience. So how will you use this miraculous life?

With the tools you've explored and the insights you've gained, you have the capacity to be a rooted renegade. You can create a fully conscious, empowered life. By boldly stepping into your gifts and unique beingness, you can generate deep fulfillment and joy on your own terms. Watch as the changes on the inside ripple out to your family, relationships, workplace, and community.

The world needs your boldness, creative expression, and full unleashed-ness to seed disruptions that heal. This is an invitation to step bravely into that, even when it feels clumsy, risky, and countercultural.

This will not be easy. You will confront internal and external resistance. You will be tempted by the easier path of the status quo and the lull of inertia. You will face self-doubt and exhaustion. You will wonder if it's all worth it.

Life is simpler when we avoid taking responsibility for our lives and go along without making waves in systems that aren't really working. But is inertia your legacy? It sure isn't mine. I'm guessing that you'd choose hard but right over complacency any day. Are you ready to lean all the way into your renegade spirit, knowing that you have a foundation of peace to come home to?

And as you embody being unleashed, you just might start to notice that you attract like-minded folks who are ready to claim life on their own terms, generating the conditions for a groundswell of authentic, powerful, rooted renegades. What a future you could create!

Practice and support are required, of course. We all have tender spots that make it hard to do the work of renegading. Most recently, mine was hearing a hateful speech about blocking teens' access to gender-affirming care. My heart dropped and my throat tightened. Then the sweat of rage came. My brain churned with arguments about trampling trans children's rights, the dehumanization of trans people, and the futility of rationality amid hate. I allowed the tears to come and slept off my anger. Then I got to the business of supporting my loved ones.

I'm learning every day, and you are too. We are always in the process of becoming the next version of ourselves.

Please don't put this book down until you've started to take concrete actions toward the life you're yearning to live. *Insights yield nothing without action.*

Rooted peace for your renegade spirit is on the other side. Remember that you can return again and again to the concepts here whenever it serves you. And if you want more resources and support, check out my website www.therootedrenegade.com and get connected with other folks doing the work. I hope you have experienced this book as a guide, a nudge, even a full-throated holler to enjoy peace of your own making.

ACKNOWLEDGMENTS

People say that writing a book is like giving birth. If so, this book was a ten-pound baby beast. Whoa. I used many of the tools and techniques in this book to support me during the process: employing the 4–7–8 Breath in the middle of long nights, connecting with my legacy when I felt down, using positive self-talk, invoking my inner pit crew, and so much more. And I broke a lifelong pattern of feeling like I need to do hard things alone. I had help from so many experts, colleagues, teachers, friends, and family that it makes me teary thinking about it.

I deeply value others' privacy, so I'm using first names only to express my gratitude for so many of you. Y'all know who you are. Thank you to my editors, Amanda, Caitlin, Claudia, Erin, Morgan, and Pam. You each bring a different lens and skill set, and the book would be a shadow of itself without you. Adrianna, thanks for keeping the whole process running smoothly. Many thanks to the entire team at Greenleaf Book Group for their unwavering support, dedication, expertise, and generosity. I hemmed and hawed about which publisher to choose, and I'm so grateful I chose you. To my incredible readers, Adrienne, Bonnie, Elisa, Laura, Lynsey, thanks for taking your own time to share your generous feedback and support. To my genius photographer, styling, and makeup "yacht" team, Brie, Kerilynn, and Steph, you made me look and feel my absolute best!

Thanks to my many, many supportive family members, friends, and colleagues. Allegra, Allison, Amy, Andrea, Audrey, Cat, Dale, Doug, Drew, Emily, Jamie, John, Juanita, Greta, Kellie and Kelly, Kelsey, Laura, Liz, Martha, Mary, Sarah, Sheila, Tracy, and Yuko, thank you for the encouragement, nudges, and texts. Special shout-out to my coach buddy, Rachel, who pushed me to finish when I had a book version of a dark night of the soul. Mom, I feel your pride even if you can't express it right now. Thank you for always wanting the best for me.

To my zany, amazing family: You endured lots of takeout, grumpy mom moments, editing blitz weekends, book talks at the dinner table, title brainstorms, and nuggets of personal development (too often). Kids: I'm lucky to be your mom. I admire your courage in becoming more and more yourselves every day. To Perry, my dearest husband who helped with everything from photoshoot prep to taking the kids for the weekend to reassuring me that this work matters when I felt down (and picking up dumplings). You are the best decision I ever made. Thanks for being the Yoda of optimism, unconditional love, and play for me.

Finally, to my courageous, brilliant clients. You astound me with your vulnerability, willingness to experiment with new ways of being in the world, and bravery in claiming what you want and not settling for the status quo. You have me racing to my desk for the privilege of speaking with you. You have taught me so much about possibility, trust, connection, and the power of having an ally on our side. Thank you for trusting me with your deepest fears and desires, allowing me to walk beside you, and relishing the sweet, tender, and hilarious moments of life together.

NOTES

CHAPTER 1

1. Amanda Blake, *Your Body Is Your Brain: Leverage Your Somatic Intelligence to Find Purpose, Build Resilience, Deepen Relationships and Lead More Powerfully* (Seattle: Embright, 2019), 55–58; Bessel Van Der Kolk, *The Body Keeps the Score: Brain, Mind, and Body in the Healing of Trauma* (London: Penguin, 2014), 94, 97–98; Alan Fogel, "Three States of Embodied Self-Awareness: The Therapeutic Vitality of Restorative Embodied Self-Awareness," *International Body Psychotherapy Journal* 19, no. 1 (Spring/Summer 2020): 39–49, https://www.ibpj.org/issues/articles/Alan%20Fogel%20-%20Three%20States%20of%20Embodied%20Self-Awareness.pdf.

2. See: Blake, *Your Body Is Your Brain*, 118; Amy Cuddy, "Your Body Language May Shape Who You Are," TED Talks, June 2012, https://www.ted.com/talks/amy_cuddy_your_body_language_may_shape_who_you_are?language=en.

3. "Your ability to feel the sensations that underlie your emotions is critical to both connection and compassion." Blake, *Your Body Is Your Brain*, 187.

4. Adapted from practices used by Amanda Blake in *Your Body Is Your Brain*, 53.

5. Blake, *Your Body Is Your Brain*, 57.

CHAPTER 2

1. You can find an example at Greater Good Science Center: https://ggia.berkeley.edu/practice/gratitude_meditation.

2. Rick Hanson discusses the H.E.A.L. method for taking in the good and generating positivity: "Have a beneficial experience"; "Enrich it"—make the experience last by thinking about it for a time; "Absorb it"—allow your whole body to take in the experience fully; "Link positive and negative material." *Being Well* podcast, https://www.rickhanson.net/well-podcast-h-e-a-l-yourself/; Rick Hanson, *Hardwiring Happiness: The New Brain Science of Contentment, Calm, and Confidence* (New York: Harmony Books, 2013), 60–63.

3. Donatella Di Corrado, Maria Guarnera, Francesca Vitali, Alessandro Quartiroli, and Marinella Coco, "Imagery Ability of Elite Level Athletes from Individual vs. Team and Contact vs. No-Contact Sports," *PeerJ* 7 (May 22, 2019): e6940, doi:10.7717/peerj.6940.

4. Lisa Feldman Barrett, "Try These Two Smart Techniques to Master Your Emotions," TED Ideas, June 21, 2018, https://ideas.ted.com/try-these-two-smart-techniques-to-help-you-master-your-emotions/; sections of this exercise are adapted from Amanda Blake's *Your Body Is Your Brain*, 255; Martha Beck, *The Way of Integrity: Finding the Path to Your True Self* (London: Piatkus, 2021), 28–30.

5. Hanson, *Hardwiring Happiness*, 91–110.

6. Derek Rydall, *The Abundance Project: 40 Days to More Wealth, Health, Love, and Happiness* (New York: Atria Books, 2022), 16–27.

7. Melissa Dahl, "A Classic Psychology Study on Why Winning the Lottery Won't Make You Happier," The Cut, January 13, 2016, https://www.thecut.com/2016/01/classic-study-on-happiness-and-the-lottery.html.

8. Adapted from Derek Rydall's *The Abundance Project*, 16–27.

9. "Frequently Asked Questions," U.S. Small Business Administration Office of Advocacy, March 2023, https://advocacy.sba.gov/wp-content/uploads/2023/03/Frequently-Asked-Questions-About-Small-Business-March-2023-508c.pdf.

10. For a detailed discussion of "swamping"—a fully embodied practice of being in your challenging emotions, including all the trappings from dress to music to who surrounds you to the items through which you express the intensity of your feelings, see: Regena Thomashauer, *Pussy: A Reclamation* (Carlsbad, CA: Hay House, 2014), 155.

11. Brené Brown, *Atlas of the Heart: Mapping Meaningful Connection and the Language of Human Experience* (New York: Random House, 2021), xxiii.

12. Yasemin Erbas, Eva Ceulemans, Madeline Lee Pe, Peter Koval, and Peter Kuppens, "Negative Emotion Differentiation: Its Personality and Well-Being Correlates and a Comparison of Different Assessment Methods," *Cognition and Emotion* 28, no. 7 (2014): 1196–1213, doi:10.1080/02699931.2013.875890.

13. For an in-depth discussion of ways to create new habits and extinguish habits that aren't serving you, see: James Clear, *Atomic Habits: An Easy and Proven Way to Build Good Habits and Break Bad Ones* (New York: Random House Business Books, 2015); Robert Kegan and Lisa Laskow Lahey, *Immunity to Change: How to Overcome It and Unlock the Potential in Yourself and Your Organization* (Boston: Harvard Business Review Press, 2009); BJ Fogg, *Tiny Habits: The Small Changes That Change Everything* (New York: Houghton Mifflin Harcourt, 2020).

CHAPTER 3

1. Based on Maslow's hierarchy of needs, originally published: A.H. Maslow, "A Theory of Human Motivation," *Psychological Review* 50, no. 4 (1943): 370–396, https://psycnet.apa.org/doi/10.1037/h0054346.

2. Draws on Maslow's hierarchy of needs, originally published: Maslow, "A Theory of Human Motivation"; Rick Hanson, *Hardwiring Happiness: The New Brain Science of Contentment, Calm, and Confidence* (New York: Harmony Books, 2013), 67–70.

3. Adapted from work by Amanda Blake, *Your Body Is Your Brain*, 129, 143–148, 155–156; Rick Hanson, *Hardwiring Happiness*, 91–110; Maslow's hierarchy of needs, originally published: Maslow, "A Theory of Human Motivation."

PART II INTRODUCTION

1. Koichiro Shiba, Laura D. Kubzansky, David R. Williams, Tyler J. VanderWeele, Eric S. Kim, "Purpose in Life and 8-Year Mortality by Gender and Race/Ethnicity Among Older Adults in the U.S.," *Preventive Medicine* 164 (November 2022): 107310, https://doi.org/10.1016/j.ypmed.2022.107310; Stacey M. Schaefer, Jennifer Morozink Boylan, Carien M. van Reekum, Regina C. Lapate, Catherine J. Norris, Carol D. Ryff, and Richard J. Davidson, "Purpose in Life Predicts Better Emotional Recovery from Negative Stimuli," *PLoS One* 8, no. 11 (November 2013): e80329, doi:10.1371/journal.pone.0080329.

CHAPTER 5

1. Simon Sinek, ethnographer, renowned TED speaker, and author has made it his life's work to help organizations, leaders, and individuals connect with the compelling power of identifying, owning, and starting with their "why." See his book: Simon Sinek, *Find Your Why: A Practical Guide for Discovering Purpose for You and Your Team* (Edmonton, Alberta: Portolio, 2017); Simon Sinek, "Start with Why—How Great Leaders Inspire Action," TEDx Talks, accessed October 23, 2023, https://www.youtube.com/watch?v=u4ZoJKF_VuA.

2. "Mihaly Csikszentmihalyi: Flow, the Secret to Happiness," YouTube, accessed November 5, 2023, https://www.youtube.com/watch?v=fXIeFJCqsPs.

3. Jen Bailey, "What We Inherit & What We Send Forth," *On Being* podcast with Krista Tippett, July 19, 2021, https://onbeing.org/programs/jen-bailey-what-we-inherit-what-we-send-forth/.

4. Janine Thome, Maria Densmore, Georgia Koppe, Braeden Terpou, Jean Théberge, Margaret C. McKinnon, and Ruth A. Lanius, "Back to the Basics: Resting State Functional Connectivity of the Reticular Activation System in PTSD and Its Dissociative Subtype," *Chronic Stress* 3 (2019), doi:10.1177/2470547019873663.

5. Adapted from work by the Co-Active Training Institute and CRR Global's Organization and Relationship Systems Coaching (ORSC™).

6. Héctor García and Francesc Miralles, *Ikigai, The Japanese Secret to a Long and Happy Life* (New York: Penguin, 2017).

7. Building New York City urban miniatures was one man's unexpected stroke of genius. This is such a specific skill set. Just imagine the possibilities for genius. See: Lizza Weisstuch, "Jobless, Divorced and on Probation, a Pandemic Hobby Turned His Life Around," *New York Times*, September 8, 2023, https://www.nytimes.com/2023/09/08/nyregion/ice-box-model-nyc.html?smid=nytcore-ios-share&referringSource=articleShare.

8. *Coaches Rising* podcast, episode 81, February 15, 2021.

9. Gay Hendricks, *The Big Leap: Conquer Your Hidden Fear and Take Life to the Next Level* (New York: HarperOne, 2009), 34.

10. Hendricks, *The Big Leap*, 33–36.

11. These questions build upon Gay Hendricks's process in *The Big Leap*, 122–141.

12. Adapted from work by David Bedrick, an author, teacher, attorney, and psychologist who focuses on unshaming parts of us that have been ostracized so we can see the beauty, resourcefulness, and brilliance that resides there; he posits that jealousy signals an area of our brilliance. And from Simone Seol and David Bedrick, course guidebook for The Shame Clinic for Entrepreneurs, Fall 2022, 60–63, https://www.simonegraceseol.com/masterclass-shame-clinic.

13. Via Institute on Character (website), accessed September 21, 2023, https://www.viacharacter.org.

14. Adapted from the work of the Co-Active Training Institute.

CHAPTER 6

1. BJ Fogg, *Tiny Habits: The Small Changes That Change Everything* (New York: Houghton Mifflin Harcourt, 2020), 139–161.

2. Adapted from work by Rick Hanson, a psychologist and senior fellow at UC Berkeley's Greater Good Science Center. He talks about allowing yourself to hold on to positive experiences and letting them sink into you. See: https://www.rickhanson.net/take-in-the-good/; Rick Hanson, Shauna Shapiro, Emma Hutton-Thamm, Michael R. Hagerty, Kevin P. Sullivan, "Learning to Learn from Positive Experiences," *The Journal of Positive Psychology* 18, no. 1 (2023): 142–153, doi:10.1080/17439760.2021.2006759; Rick Hanson, *Hardwiring Happiness: The New Brain Science of Contentment, Calm, and Confidence* (New York: Harmony Books, 2013), 76–90.

3. Jack Canfield, *The Success Principles: How to Get from Where You Are to Where You Want to Be* (Boston, MA: Mariner Books, 2015), 154–155.

4. Julie Tseng and Jordan Poppenk, "Brain Meta-State Transitions Demarcate Thoughts Across Task Contexts Exposing the Mental Noise of Trait Neuroticism," *Nature Communications* 11, no. 3480 (July 13, 2020), https://doi.org/10.1038/s41467-020-17255-9.

5. Robert C. Wilson, Amitai Shenhav, Mark Straccia, and Jonathan D. Cohen, "The Eighty-Five Percent Rule for Optimal Learning," *Nature Communications* 10, no. 4646 (November 5, 2019), https://doi.org/10.1038/s41467-019-12552-4.

6. R. Douglas Fields, "The Brain Learns in Unexpected Ways," *Scientific American*, March 1, 2020, https://www.scientificamerican.com/article/the-brain-learns-in-unexpected-ways/.

7. *Chef's Table*, "Dario Cecchini," season 6, episode 2, https://www.imdb.com/title/tt9675418/.

8. Adapted from work by the Co-Active Training Institute.

9. Fogg, *Tiny Habits*, 139–161.

10. If you regularly self-sabotage, see: Robert Kegan and Lisa Laskow Lahey, *Immunity to Change: How to Overcome It and Unlock the Potential in Yourself and Your Organization* (Boston: Harvard Business Review Press, 2009). The authors delve into ways to understand the "hidden competing commitments" and "big assumptions" we hold that subvert our goals.

CHAPTER 7

1. Adapted from work by the Co-Active Training Institute.

2. Draws on elements of the Internal Family Systems model of psychotherapy and work by the Co-Active Training Institute.

3. For a deep dive into the internal saboteurs that undermine our efforts, see: "How We Self Sabotage," Positive Intelligence, accessed October 23, 2023, https://www.positiveintelligence.com/saboteurs/.

4. Adapted from work by the Co-Active Training Institute.

5. Draws on elements of the Internal Family Systems model of psychotherapy and work by the Co-Active Training Institute.

6. Saul McLeod, "Maslow's Hierarchy of Needs," Simply Psychology, updated October 18, 2023, https://www.simplypsychology.org/maslow.html.

7. Adapted from work by Amanda Blake, *Your Body Is Your Brain: Leverage Your Somatic Intelligence to Find Purpose, Build Resilience, Deepen Relationships and Lead More Powerfully* (Seattle: Embright, 2019), 255.

8. Martin R. Huecker, Jacob Shreffler, Patrick T. McKeny, and David Davis, *Imposter Syndrome* (Treasure Island, FL: StatPearls, 2023), https://www.ncbi.nlm.nih.gov/books/NBK585058.

9. Draws on elements of the Internal Family Systems model of psychotherapy, work by the Co-Active Training Institute, and Positive Intelligence (https://www.positiveintelligence.com).

10. Draws on elements of the Internal Family Systems model of psychotherapy and work by the Co-Active Training Institute.

11. "Defrosting the Wild Animal Inside You with David Bedrick," *I Am Your Korean Mom*, episode 207, September 11, 2022, https://podcasts. apple.com/us/podcast/207-defrosting-the-wild-animal-inside-you-with/ id1480776334?i=1000579110313; "Shamanic Shape-Shifting with David Bedrick," *I Am Your Korean Mom*, episode 208, September 12, 2022, https://podcasts.apple.com/us/podcast/i-am-your-korean-mom/ id1480776334?i=1000579231926.

12. David Bedrick, "UnShamed TV Episode One: UnShaming Performance Anxiety," YouTube, accessed November 5, 2023, https://www.youtube.com/ watch?v=eyps2aGwhNA.

13. Richard Boyatzis and Kleio Akrivou, "The Ideal Self as the Driver of Intentional Change," *Journal of Management Development* 25, no. 7 (August 2006): 624–642, doi:10.1108/02621710610678454.

14. James Clear, *Atomic Habits: An Easy and Proven Way to Build Good Habits and Break Bad Ones* (New York: Random House Business Books, 2015), 33, 36, 38.

15. Clear, *Atomic Habits*, 33: "The ultimate form of intrinsic motivation is when a habit becomes part of your identity. It's one thing to say I'm the type of person who wants this. It's something very different to say I'm the type of person who is this." P. 36: "Your habits are how you embody your identity." P. 38: "The most practical way to change who you are is to change what you do."

16. Jack Canfield, *The Success Principles: How to Get from Where You Are to Where You Want to Be* (Boston, MA: Mariner Books, 2015), 123–132.

CHAPTER 8

1. See: *Our Epidemic of Loneliness and Isolation: The U.S. Surgeon General's Advisory on the Healing Effects of Social Connection and Community* (2023), accessed October 23, 2023, https://www.hhs.gov/sites/default/files/surgeon-general-social-connection-advisory.pdf

2. "Envy occurs when we want something that another person has." Brené Brown, *Atlas of the Heart: Mapping Meaningful Connection and the Language of Human Experience* (New York: Random House, 2021), 25; Brown quotes a 2015 study finding that 90 percent of envious moments relate to attractiveness, competence, or wealth (Katrin Rentzsch and James J. Gross, "Who Turns Green with Envy? Conceptual and Empirical Perspectives on Dispositional Envy," *European Journal of Personality* 29, no. 5 (2015): 530–547, https://doi.org/10.1002/per.2012.)

3. For a deep dive into criticism and "unhooking" from praise and criticism, see: Tara Mohr, *Playing Big: Practical Wisdom for Women Who Want to Speak Up, Create, and Lead* (New York: Avery, 2015), 89–121.

4. For more detail about types of boundaries, ways to set boundaries, how to troubleshoot boundary incursions, see: Nedra Glover Tawwab: *Set Boundaries, Find Peace: A Guide to Reclaiming Yourself* (London: Piatkus, 2021).

5. This is an example of nonviolent communication. Marshall Rosenberg, *Living Nonviolent Communication: Practical Tools to Connect and Communicate Skillfully in Every Situation* (Boulder: Sounds True, 2012), xi.

6. Rosenberg, *Living Nonviolent Communication,* xi.

7. Adapted from work by the Co-Active Training Institute.

8. Ming Zhang, Yuqi Zhang, and Yazhuo Kong, "Interaction between Social Pain and Physical Pain," *Brain Science Advances* 5, no. 4 (2019): 265–273, doi:10.26599/BSA.2019.9050023; Data shows that loneliness impacts our mortality. See: Maria Morava and Scottie Andrew, "Loneliness Won't End When the Pandemic Ends," CNN.com, April 17, 2021, https://www.cnn.com/2021/04/17/us/loneliness-epidemic-covid-wellness-trnd/index.html.

9. Jack Canfield, *The Success Principles: How to Get from Where You Are to Where You Want to Be* (Boston, MA: Mariner Books, 2015), 227; Aimee Groth, "You're the Average of the Five People You Spend the Most Time With," Business Insider, July 24, 2012, https://www.businessinsider.com/jim-rohn-youre-the-average-of-the-five-people-you-spend-the-most-time-with-2012-7.

10. The Center for Nonviolent Communication, https://www.cnvc.org/; The Gottman Institute, https://www.gottman.com/.

11. This is a rich cultural practice about which I am not an expert. I invite you to explore further if you are interested to understand the roots and complexity of this powerful tradition. See these resources from Dr. James, an academic of Hawaiian descent who has studied the impact of *Ho'oponopono*: "Sample Huna: Ho'oponopono," Huna, accessed October 23, 2023, https://www.huna.com/process-of-hooponopono/; Dr. Matt James, "7-Minute Ho'oponopono Forgiveness Process with Dr. Matt James," YouTube, accessed October 23, 2023, https://youtu.be/FaMcgtswmVA; Matt James, "The Hawaiian Secret of Forgiveness," *Psychology Today*, May 23, 2011, https://www.psychologytoday.com/us/blog/focus-forgiveness/201105/

the-hawaiian-secret-forgiveness; Matthew B. James, "Ho'oponopono: Assessing the Effects of a Traditional Hawaiian Forgiveness Technique on Unforgiveness" (PhD diss., Walden University, 2008), https://scholarworks.waldenu.edu/dissertations/622/.

12. Denise Duffield-Thomas, *Get Rich, Lucky Bitch!: Release Your Money Blocks and Live a First-Class Life* (Carlsbad, CA: Hay House, 2013).

CHAPTER 9

1. Adapted from CRR Global's Organization and Relationship Systems Coaching (ORSC™).

2. Oliver Burkeman, *Four Thousand Weeks: Time Management for Mortals* (New York: Farrar, Straus and Giroux, 2021). This is an excellent exploration of our conceptions of time.

3. Gay Hendricks, *The Big Leap: Conquer Your Hidden Fear and Take Life to the Next Level* (New York: HarperOne, 2009), 176.

4. Brené Brown, *Atlas of the Heart: Mapping Meaningful Connection and the Language of Human Experience* (New York: Random House, 2021), 59. Brown cites: Dacher Keltner, "Why do We Feel Awe?" *Greater Good Magazine: Science-Based Insights for a Meaningful Life*, May 10, 2016, https://greatergood.berkeley.edu/article/item/why_do_we_feel_awe; Jennifer E. Stellar, Amie Gordon, Craig L. Anderson, Paul K. Piff, Galen D. McNeil, and Dacher Keltner, "Awe and Humility," *Journal of Personality and Social Psychology* 114, no. 2 (2018): 258–269, doi:10.1037/pspi0000109.

5. If you're interested in learning about the life-altering impacts of awe, see: Dacher Keltner, *Awe: The New Science of Everyday Wonder and How It Can Transform Your Life* (New York: Penguin Press, 2023).

6. "The Neural Basis of Confirmation Bias," *Neuroscience News*, December 18, 2019, https://neurosciencenews.com/confirmation-bias-15327/; Janine Thome, Maria Densmore, Georgia Koppe, Braeden Terpou, Jean Théberge, Margaret C. McKinnon, and Ruth A. Lanius, "Back to the Basics: Resting State Functional Connectivity of the Reticular Activation System in PTSD and Its Dissociative Subtype," *Chronic Stress* 3 (2019), doi:10.1177/2470547019873663.

CHAPTER 10

1. *Netflix's Myths & Monsters*, "Heroes & Villains," season 1, episode 1, https://www.youtube.com/watch?v=DwnxYXOTy94.

CHAPTER 11

1. Marshall Rosenberg, *Living Nonviolent Communication: Practical Tools to Connect and Communicate Skillfully in Every Situation* (Boulder: Sounds True, 2012). This book provides a framework for how to share your needs with others and navigate disruption in life-affirming ways.

2. Christiana Figueres, "Ecological Hope, and Spiritual Evolution," *On Being* podcast with Krista Tippett, November 9, 2023, https://onbeing.org/programs/christiana-figueres-ecological-hope-and-spiritual-evolution/.

ABOUT THE AUTHOR

Rebecca Arnold, JD, CPCC, PCC, is a professional, certified coach and the founder of Root Coaching & Consulting, LLC, a holistic leadership coaching firm. Her clients are mission-driven leaders in the fields of education, medicine, law, academia, and social-impact organizations. An attorney by training, Rebecca has a background in education policy. She was a presidential management fellow at the US Department of Education and a special assistant to the Assistant Secretary for Career, Technical, and Adult Education. In those positions, she focused on reform initiatives for high schools and community colleges. She has worked with numerous social-impact organizations in the education and social justice arenas. She holds a JD from Northeastern University and a BA from Brown University.

But more importantly, she's known as a "straight-talkin', big-hearted" coach. In addition, Rebecca is a dog mom, a mom to teens, and a spunky wife. To access her own essence, she practices yoga, meditates, uses Reiki, walks by the ocean, cooks without recipes, sits in coffee shops, peruses plant shops, and laughs like hell. See what Rebecca's up to at rootcoachingconsulting.com and find her @rootcoach on Instagram.